THE STEERSMAN

METABELIEFS
AND SELF-NAVIGATION

by John C. Lilly, M.D.

Translated by Beverly A. Potter, Ph.D.

Ronin Publishing, Inc.

Berkeley, California

www.roninpub.com

THE STEERSMAN

METABELIEFS AND SELF-NAVIGATION

by John C. Lilly, M.D.

Translated by Beverly A. Potter, Ph.D.

The Steersman

Copyright: 1956, 1958, 1960, 1961, 1969, 1975, John C. Lilly, M.D.

Derivative Copyright 2007 by Beverly A. Potter

& Philip Hansen Bailey Lilly

ISBN: 1-57951-037-X; 978-1-57951-037-4

Published by

Ronin Publishing, Inc.

PO Box 22900

Oakland, CA 94609

www.roninpub.com

Production:

Editor: Beverly A. Potter (docpotter.com)

Cover Design: Brian Groppe (briangroppe.com)

Book Design: Beverly A. Potter

Fonts:

Steamer, Book Antique, Copperplate

Library of Congress Card Number: 2007923934

Distributed to the book trade by **Publishers Group West**

Printed in the United States by Inner Workings

NOTE: Material in this book was derived from *Simulations of God: The Science of Belief*

ACKNOWLEDGEMENTS

Thanks to John and Colette Lilly of Zacatecas, Mexico. Ann and Jerry Moss of The Moss Foundation for their assistance in digitizing the scientific and medical research papers of Dr. John C. Lilly, and making them available on the world wide web. The extended Lilly family: Lisa Lyon Lilly, Barbara Clarke Lilly, Cynthia Lilly Cantwell, Nina Lilly Castellucio, Charles Richard Lilly, and Mary Louise Lilly. Faustin Bray of Soundphotosnthesis, Mill Valley, California, for continuing to make the multimedia legacy of Dr. Lilly available to all. Patricia Sims and James Suhre, Board Directors of the John C. Lilly Research Institute, Inc. Star Newland and Dr. Michael Hyson of the Cetacean Commonwealth, Sirius Institute, Planet Puna, Pahoa, Hawaii, for their continuing support of Dr. Lilly's consciousness research projects. Robert Goodman of Hilo, Hawaii, for her expansion of interspecies communication with Cetacea. Napier Marten and Ian Middleton of the band, Cetacea, for their a multi-media project in support of dolphin and whale conservation. Dr. Paul and Helena Spong at Orca Lab, Hansen Island, British Columbia, continuing their research into Orca habitat research. Tango Snyder and John Allen at the Institute of Ecotechnics. Bigtwin, creator and designer of the official John C. Lilly website, along with his partner Kate Greene. Furthermore to Dr. Lawrence and Charlene Raithaus, Brian Wallace, Bob Von Lowe, Denise Smith, Adam Keith, Gerard Houghton, Divyam Preaux, Jean Francois Simmonet, Rio and Teresa Hahn, Kim and Jim Ed Norman, and George and Evelyn Musser for their continued support. Glenn and Lee Perry, Samdhi Tank Company, Grass Valley, California, designers and purveyors of the Lilly inspired isolation tanks.

Dedicated to **Philip Hansen Bailey** for his determined work on my behalf for nearly twenty years. Philip's close personal and professional relationship with me gives him a unique insight into my life and work. His perseverance in the publication of these works provides for the enjoyment of new generations of seekers and voyagers, and is a boon for us all.

TABLE OF CONTENTS

PREFACE

I **wish to tell you,** my reader, what it is, who I am, who they are, when and where. I wish but cannot tell the truth, objectively. In me are an editor, a judge, a jury, a missionary, a rebel, several small children, a woman, a man, parents, a small heaven, a large hell, and various spirits, witches, goblins, saints, sinners, heroes, a scientist, a lover, and a fear of this crowd. The fear is that I'll go under, be lost as one or another of these crowdy "me's" gains control over poor little me, the real me crouching afraid in the corner of this roomy head on my body.

Somewhere there must be a real me: the one who gives in to the judge and jury, the one who listens and becomes the contrite sinner as the judge pronounces sentence. Escaping judgment, am I the missionary, secure in fantasied virtue, proclaiming the mission for the rest? The rebel, skeptical, dissents from the mission. Which is the true me? The rebel disclaiming or the missionary proclaiming? I've preached, rebelled, and preached, and then researched the mission. The scientist, safe in my fantasied objectivity, researching that outside myself, pushing my mission on others, preaching a new science here and a new science there. Am I he? Making science judgments now?

The human software for changing belief systems, expanding them, opening them up and incorporating the unknown as part of our belief systems is becoming available. The investigation of this human software is a proper science expanded beyond the current so-called natural sciences, within the sciences of mathematics, of theoretical physics and of states of consciousness. What I am presenting is a "true/as if true" science of belief.

To investigate my own belief systems, I used the tool of solitude, isolation, and confinement in a silent dark tank of fifteen percent saline solution. In solitude I could see very clearly after several hours of exposure where my belief systems were; what I believed to be true, to be real, to be unequivocally correct, trustworthy, reliable, certain.

PLEASE KEEP IN MIND THAT THIS WORK IS A SIMULATION, EVEN AS YOU ARE TO ME AND I AM TO YOU.

Man is the animal that simulates reality and believes that simulation. Please keep in mind that this work is a simulation, even as you are to me and I am to you. This is a handbook to start you on your search for your beliefs — your personal simulations — that define your realities. It is a long search, involving much research. In this book you will find some of the supra-self-metaprograms that regulate our lives and which might prove helpful as a starting point.

Our simulations control our thinking, our feelings, and our actions. Until we learn otherwise we are the victim, the slave, the agonist of our simulations. The simulations we make of our self can, upon deep analysis, be shown to be largely emergency fire drill dictates from the past. In the early years the excitation of our survival programs tends to dictate the definition of our simulations of self. This may not be all we are but for purposes of the bodily planet-side trip it's a large fraction of the biocomputer's content and control systems.

PART ONE

HOW METABELIEFS ARE PROGRAMMED

PROGRAMMABLE BIOCOMPUTER

All **human beings,** all persons who reach adulthood are programmed biocomputers. We cannot escape our nature as a programmable entity. Literally, each of us may be our programs, nothing more, nothing less. Despite the great varieties available, most of us have a limited set of programs. Some are built-in — hard wired.

The structure of our nervous system reflects its origins in simpler forms of organisms, from sessile protozoans, sponges, and corals through sea worms, reptiles and protomammals to primates to early anthropoids to humanoids to man. In the simpler basic forms the programs were mostly built-in from genetic codes to fully formed organisms adult reproducing, the patterns of function of action-reaction were determined by necessities of survival, of adaptation to slow environmental changes, of passing on the codes to descendants.

As the size and complexity of the nervous system and its bodily carrier increased, new levels of programmability appeared, not tied to immediate survival and eventual reproduction. The built-in programs survive as a basic underlying context for the new levels, excitable and inhabitable by the overlying control systems. The cerebral cortex is an expanding new high-level computer controlling the structurally lower levels of the nervous system — the lower built-in programs. As the cortex expanded over several millions of years, a critical size of cortex was reached and a new level of structure, a new capability emerged: *learning to learn.*

Learning to Learn

When we learn to learn, we make models, use symbols, analogize, create metaphors to invent and use language, mathematics, art, politics, business, and so forth. Language and its consequences appeared at this critical brain cortex size,

Learning permits us to make faster adaptation to a rapidly changing environment. As we developed "metaprogramming" capability and ability to "learn" we were increasingly able to avoid having to repeat the process of using certain symbols, metaphors, models each time we encounter a particular situation. Metaprogramming appears at the critical cortical size because the cerebral computer must have a large enough number of interconnected circuits of sufficient quality for the operations of metaprogramming to exist in the biocomputer.

ALL WE ARE AS HUMANS IS WHAT IS BUILT IN AND WHAT HAS BEEN ACQUIRED AND WHAT WE MAKE OF BOTH OF THESE.

Metaprogramming

Metaprogramming is an operation in which a central control system controls hundreds of thousands of programs that simultaneously operate in parallel. Man-made computers have not yet achieved this operating capacity, by the way. Metaprogramming is done outside the computer by the human programmer or, more properly, the human metaprogrammer. All choices and assignments the computer does, — how it operates, what goes into it — is still human biocomputer choices.

When I said that we may be our programs, nothing more, nothing less, I meant that the basic substrate, the substrate under all else, of our metaprograms in our system of programs — our basic operating system — runs the biovehicle. All we are as humans is what is built in — what has been acquired and what we make of these. So we are a result of the program substrate — the self-metaprogrammer.

Who is the Steersman?

Out of several hundreds of thousands of the substrate programs comes an adaptable changing set of thousands of metaprograms, so out of the metaprograms as substrate comes something else: the controller — the steersman, the programmer in the biocomputer, the self-metaprogrammer. In a well-organized biocomputer, there is a critical control metaprogram labeled "I" for acting on other metaprograms and labeled "me" when acted upon by other metaprograms. Most of us

THE STEERSMAN IS THE PROGRAMMER IN THE BIOCOMPUTER, THE SELF-METAPROGRAMMER.

have several controllers or "selves" — self-metaprograms, which divide control among them, in sequences of control, either parallel in time or in series.

The Self-Metaprogrammer

Self-development is the centralizing of control of your biocomputer in your self-metaprogrammer, making the others into conscious executives subordinate to the single administrator — the single superconscient self-metaprogrammer. With appropriate methods, this centralizing of control, the elementary unification operation is a realizable state for many, if not all, biocomputers.

Supraself-Metaprograms

Beyond and above in the control hierarchy, the position of this single administrative self-metaprogrammer and its staff, there may be other controls and controllers which I call "supraself-metaprograms". These are many or one, depending on current consciousness in the single self-metaprogrammer. These may be personified "as if" entities, treated "as if" a network for information transfer, or a "realized as if" self traveling in the universe to strange lands or dimensions or spaces. At times we are tempted to pull together apparently independent supraself sources "as if" one.

WE ARE GENERAL-PURPOSE COMPUTERS, WHICH CAN PROGRAM ANY CONCEIVABLE MODEL OF THE UNIVERSE INSIDE OUR OWN STRUCTURE.

We are general purpose computers who can program any conceivable model of the universe inside our own structure, reduce the single self-metaprogrammer to a micro size, and program him — or her — to travel through his own model "as if" real. This ability is useful when we step outside it and see it for what it is — an immensely satisfying realization of the programmatic power of our biocomputer. Realizing that we have this ability is an important addition to our self-metaprogrammatic list of probables.

When we have control over modeling the universe inside our self and are able to vary the parameters satisfactorily, our self may reflect this ability by changing appropriately to match the new property.

The quality of our models of the universe are measured by how well they match the real universe. There is no guarantee that our current model does match the reality, no matter how certain we feel that

THE QUALITY OF OUR MODELS OF THE UNIVERSE ARE MEASURED BY HOW WELL THEY MATCH THE REAL UNIVERSE.

there is a match and that it is a match of high quality. Feelings of awe, reverence, sacredness and certainty are also adaptable metaprograms, attachable to any model, not just the one best fitting the "reality."

Modem science knows this. We know that merely because a culture generated a cosmology of a certain kind and worshipped it. There is no guarantee of its goodness of fit with the real universe. In science we proceed to test our models of the universe — insofar as they are testable — rather than to accept those models as "real". Feelings such as awe and reverence are biocomputer energy sources rather than determinants of truth, that is, of the trueness of fit of models versus realities. A pervasive feeling of certainty is recognized as a property of a state of consciousness, a special space, which may be indicative or suggestive but is not considered as a final judgment of a true fitting. Even as we can travel inside our models inside our heads, so can we travel outside or be outside of our models of the universe, and still inside our heads.

Province of the Mind

In the province of the mind, what we believe to be true either is true or becomes true within certain limits to be found experientially and experimentally. These limits are further beliefs to be transcended. In the province of mind, there are no limits.

The province of the mind is the region of our models, of the alone self, of memory, of the metaprograms. What of the region that includes our body, others' bodies? Here there are definite limits. In the network of bodies — our own connected with others' for bodily survival, procreation, and creation — there is another kind of information.

WHAT THE NETWORK BELIEVES TO BE TRUE EITHER IS TRUE OR BECOMES TRUE

In the province of connected minds, what the network believes to be true either is true or becomes true within certain limits to be found experientially and experimentally. These limits are further beliefs to be transcended. In the province of the network's mind, there are no limits.

Consensus Science

But once again the bodies of the network housing the minds, the ground on which they rest, the planet's surface, impose definite limits. These limits are to be found experientially and experimentally, agreed upon by specially trained minds and communicated to the network. This is called "consensus science".

Thus, so far we have information without limits in our mind and with agreed-upon limits, possibly unnecessary, in a network of minds. We also have information within definite limits to be found in one body and in a network of bodies on a planet.

REALITY

We are, each of us, an entity inhabiting a biochemical robot, yet we are more than the robot. I am independent of the machine, the biocomputer, the brain, and the body in which I live. I don't quite know, nor did any of the ancient philosophers know, how our consciousness inhabited a configuration of atoms and molecules. As we change the molecules, the consciousness and the realities of that consciousness change. Somehow the realities of the situation, the determinacy that generates the reality, are in the structure of the assemblage, molecules, crystals, liquid crystals, conductors, and lasers, masers, which make up the body.

We are not our whole structure. We are only inhabitants of that structure. In order to appreciate what I am talking about, you must directly experience your own simulations—your simulations of yourself, the fakeries that you place in the place of yourself. You are not your opinion of you. You are a small program in an immense space that contains billions of programs. You are one among many, the part of the whole.

As we discover inside ourselves how we are built, we can build simulations of ourselves outside ourselves. We then can produce, can create from the raw materials of the mother earth planet very peculiar forms—solid state, liquid state, gas state, gel state, and so forth—replications, models, simulations of ourselves, extensions of ourselves. We move about with them, we become mobile with them. We use the energy, the entropic energy of dead animals, of dead plants, on a network of interrelated and interconnected lines of communication in a huge hive of human activities.

WE ARE AN ENTITY INHABITING A BIOCHEMICAL ROBOT, YET WE ARE MORE THAN THE ROBOT.

What is Real?

Early Romans used the word "res" —a lawcourt—to express what appeared to them the *most real object.* A law-court in their time meant the power to judge over life and death, family and possessions, in short, over everything that comprised their existence. Ancient Roman minds couldn't quite express the meaning of our word "reality," so they used this appropriate word to signify the most positive fact of their life.

Through successive generations res gradually assumed the meaning of the modern word "thing" —an object of thought. Thing itself in the original Anglo-Saxon and Teutonic meant law-court. So we find two separate primitive peoples expressing their conception of reality by a law-court. Reality has evolved directly from these concepts.

Inner and Outer Realities

Independent realities exist, which do not depend upon our belief systems. We project simulations on to these realities, thus confusing what we

wish the universe to be with what it is. The science of
the outer realities and the science of the inner realities
are each postulated and constructed by the observer. If
in our simulations, our models, our ideas, our thinking machinery as modified by contact with the universe, we see the way through the discipline of the external realities to the discipline of the internal realities,
then as a person, we can become complete, instead of
a half-person—an inner person or an outer person.

Women seem to have fewer problems with examining, appreciating, savoring and living within the
internal realities. Their problems lie in overextending
the laws of the inner realities on to the outer realities.
By contrast, men tend to overextend the laws of external realities on to the inner realities. And yet both
male or yang and female or yin energies complete our
experience of inner and outer realities. Truth for observers lies in yin truth and yang truth—female truth
and male truth, which are reciprocally, complimenta-
rily related, one to the other, completing the universe
of simulations, of experience and of experiment. With
deep reflection, each of us can find both male and
female in ourselves.

Ignorance

We attempt to subsume in our belief
systems a complete picture of reality, of the universe,
of God, as if we knew it all. Of course, this is false.
We are proud of our knowledge and ashamed of our
ignorance. We should have neither shame nor pride
in regard to our knowledge. Our knowledge just is.
Our ignorance just is. If we can shed all preconcep-
tions, including the psychoanalytic ones, and think of
ourselves in terms of our structure, of our quantum
mechanics, of our quantum mechanical minimum possible operators, minimum possible observers, minimum possible choosers, minimum possible others, we

can then build up a structure, an analog, a metaphor of ourselves which is more in keeping with what is actually there.

Objective Reality?

Reality may be said in its less involved meanings to possess the same attributes as the original meaning of res. First, it expresses that which is completely objective as opposed to anything subjective. By objective, we mean existing without the mind, outside it, and wholly independent of it. Subjective, on the other hand, involves that which is in the mind. For instance, consider the case of a small child whose fingers have been stepped on. The child perceives through its sense of sight that a thing has caused a sensation of pain, also that this was not under control of its mind, therefore it is objective. The sensation of pain passing to the child's brain forms a thought of fear or anger directed towards the cause of the sensation. This thought is subjective.

OBJECTIVE: EXISTING WITHOUT THE MIND, OUTSIDE IT, AND WHOLLY INDEPENDENT OF IT. SUBJECTIVE: THAT WHICH IS IN THE MIND

From this prime meaning of reality many subjective ones have arisen. Consider two cases, one being a man who is a genius working on an original problem, such as the quantum theory; and one of a young man intensely in love for the first time. The genius concentrates on his problem to such an extent that he entirely forgets, or puts aside his environment. The only real existence this man has is in his mind.

It is practically the same in the situation of the young man who is so perfectly under the influence of the captivation of the girl that he thrusts aside everything but thoughts of her. He is controlled, not by outside means, but by his own state of mind. He can **WHICH IS** hardly eat or sleep; he doesn't pay **MORE REAL?** attention to anything exterior to his **OBJECTIVE** thoughts. This great emotional stress is **REALITY OR** so predominant that it is now his only **SUBJECTIVE** existence and reality. **REALITY?**

Passing from this simple state of subjectivity, reality becomes involved in the question: How can the mind render itself sufficiently objective to study itself? In other words, how are we able to use the mind to ponder on the mind? It is perfectly feasible for the intellect to grasp the fact that the physiological changes of the brain occur simultaneously with thought, but it cannot conceive of the connection between its own thoughts and these changes. The difficulties of the precise relation between the two have caused many controversies as to which is the more real, the objective or the subjective reality.

Going further, let us consider an extreme case. A man is alone on a barren island with no sign of life on it. After a period of time this man begins to **HOW ARE WE** see the stark barrenness of objective **ABLE TO USE** reality; he perceives that there is **THE MIND TO** nothing for him in the world but his **PONDER ON THE** own thoughts. The question now **MIND?** arises: Is the reality the man experiences really subjective — that is, does it exist solely in his mind, or does it have an external existence?

Bishop Berkely had an interesting viewpoint on this question. He said, *"All those bodies which compose the mighty frame of the world have not any substance without the mind. So long as they are not perceived by me, or do not exist in my mind, or that of any other created spirit, they must either have no existence at all, or subsist in the mind of some Eternal Spirit."*

Bishop Berkely's reasoning takes a more philosophical view than we have been following but carries beyond where psychology has to stop. Nevertheless, the psychology of the situation agrees with this attitude.

Reality, then, resolves itself into more of a study of the intellect than of objectivity. It is possible to go still deeper in the discussion of this subject, but we will have to content ourselves with this bare scratching of the surface.

BELIEFS

Basic beliefs are basic postulates operative through long-term behavior, writings, and vocal productions of a given individual. Belief systems are those vital guides by which we steer our lives. They are rarely conscious constructions. As with an iceberg, the greater part of our guiding beliefs are below ordinary level of perception.

Systems of belief are simulations constructed by individuals, by groups, by villages, states, nations, by the united nations and embody that which is considered to be an essential guide by which to navigate our lives. Beliefs offer us a kind of certainty or determinacy in the face of the essential indeterminacy of the universe. Belief systems program into our biocomputers that which is reproducible and certain—the basic givens we believe to be true and reliable. We use these givens as guides to navigate through life.

Belief systems are analogous to garments that we can put on and take off, various colors and vari-

ous designs that may be rageous, sexual, emotional
or totally alien. As an example, I sometimes imagine
myself to be both male and female, an androgyny if

BELIEF SYSTEMS you wish. At other times I
ARE LIKE GARMENTS battle the female, pushing her
THAT WE CAN PUT back into the deep recesses
ON AND TAKE OFF, of my unconscious; at still
other times I am the female
deeply repressing the male. Only in my best thinking
can I fuse these two so that they halt their warfare and
become a neutral androgynous being, combining the
best of yin and yang, of female and male. Thus are my
belief systems generated by my being resident in a
male body in a set of circumstances on this planet.

A given belief system can be believed only when it is
appropriate to believe it. Appropriateness is determined
by ourself and the social reality in which we exist.

Belief systems are like an iceberg because about
ninety percent of them lie below our usual levels of
perception. In specifically programmed states of consciousness it is possible to become more fully aware of
our belief systems and some of their operations.

Simulation Mode

If I assume, for purposes of discussion, something to be "true" or "false", whether or not it is either,
then the assumed belief is either "as if true" or "as if
false". These beliefs are used in everyday life such as
when discussing alternative courses of future action,
for example. We have not yet entered the region of
the future action in the external world; therefore we
cannot yet say whether a given course and its consequences are "true" or "false". Instead we simulate the
alternatives and run our model of the desired action-
consequences "as if true" and check out the operations
for their "as if" values, "as if true/false".

**THE ICEBERG OF BE-
LIEF IS MOSTLY HID-
DEN, DEEP INSIDE, IN
THE INNER REALITY
THAT IS THE SEA OF
THE SELF, BECAUSE
ONLY A SMALL PART
SHOWS TO OTHERS,
A POSSIBLY LARGER
PART TO SELF.**

For purposes of understanding, we can differen-
tiate a pair of logic beliefs in addition to "true" and
"false". These are the "as if" beliefs "as if true" and
"as if false". This is the pair used when we describe or
model or represent or simulate a system.

By entering into each belief system "as if true,"
and then constructing a "reality" which is believed as
"true," we "realize" the simulation-belief system. In
leaving the belief system, we record what happened
as true and later restore the "as if true/false" values of
the simulation.

In addition to using this simulation mode in choos-
ing among alternative courses of action and their
consequences, we use it in other everyday areas. For
example, reading fiction—a sci-fi thriller, for example—we use "as if true/false". In the post-reading
period we examine the simulations for their "real"
beliefs. Have we created or learned anything exciting,
new, useful, or profound by the "simulated experience"? In this sense, a simulation, a model, a set of
programs, can be thought of as a script or scenario

for use by us or by others. The basis for responsibility and its education is found in this basic structure of the feeling-thinking machinery of the individual.

Discovering Basic Beliefs

Explore basic beliefs with me. I can, despite my own limits, point out ways to take off on your own search, directions to look in, and methods of integrating the new as you find it. One of the excitements— and it *can* be exciting—of this chase is finding truths you felt existed but didn't feel prepared to see clearly. I can, if you wish it, help you confirm your feelings for what is true in certain areas of search and research.

I do not ask that you believe me. Quite the opposite: I value my skepticism; keep yours. If you disbelieve me, watch your disbelief—it is merely another form of belief. So I do not ask you to disbelieve me either. I ask you to consider and think about what I write, make what you can yours, and let the rest go for a while. I have found that many persons can read through a book of this kind and a week, a month, a year later, discover its deeper meaning. A judicious skepticism, dispassionately held, is a good middle ground for this task.

BELIEFS ARE THE BASIC GIVEN WE ACCEPT AS TRUE AND RELIABLE. BELIEFS ARE THE BEACONS BY WHICH WE NAVIGATE THROUGH THE ROCKY WATERS OF LIFE.

Revising Basic Beliefs

The human software for changing belief systems, expanding them, opening them up and incorporating the unknown as if's of our belief systems is becoming available. Investigation of human software is a proper science expanded beyond the current so-called natural sciences, within the sciences of mathematics, of theoretical physics and of states of consciousness.

I will supply samples so that you can learn what the techniques are, what the metaprograms are, for analyzing your belief systems, and for finding out which is most important to you, yourself, within yourself, here and now. When you really start looking at these aspects of yourself, you will find that you are quite happy with certain of them but discontent with others, so that you will want to revise aspects of your basic belief systems.

You may be tempted to take one of the powerful "mind-expanding" chemical substances, like LSD or Ecstasy, to aid you as a tool in this self-analysis. Timothy Leary believed such chemical tools, sometimes called "entheogens", enable us to review and rewrite our metaprograms.

I want to emphasize that I do not encourage taking drugs except under the supervision of a doctor who has experienced far-out spaces, who has used these chemical substances and can serve as a guide as well as a safetyman under potentially dangerous circumstances. I do not advocate the use of illegal substances.

Isolation Tank

A safer way than the use of consciousness-changing drugs is to separate yourself from society while you progress through your self-examination is to use the solitude, isolation and confinement tank.

In the quest of empirical answers to these questions, I developed the technique of solitude, isolation and confinement of the essential human being in 1954 at the National Institute of Mental Health, Bethesda, Maryland, where I was doing research on the brain.

I used suspension in a water tank, in the darkness and silence. During experiments with the tank I came upon the basic beliefs of religion, science, the law, politics, in short, of the basic beliefs of all human beings.

The tank method of solitude, isolation and confinement offered me a way to be freed of the social necessities and able to take on any belief system to purposefully experience it "as if true" for a few hours and to study it at a metalevel. When I came out of the tank, I resumed the belief system appropriate to my "real life" situation at hand.

Given a single body and a single mind physically isolated and confined in a completely physically controlled environment in true solitude, with our present sciences, can we satisfactorily account for all inputs and all outputs to and from this mind-biocomputer? Can we isolate and confine them? Given the properties of the software-mind of the biocomputer outlined above, is it probable that we can find, discover, or invent inputs-outputs not yet in our consensus science? Does this center of consciousness receive-transmit information by at present unknown modes of communication? Does this center of consciousness stay in the isolated, confined biocomputer?

There are only ten inches of water in the tank, heated to 93^0 F. and with enough Epsom salts so that my hands, feet and head all float effortlessly. When I lie on my back I can breathe quite comfortably and safely, freed from sight, sound, people and the universe outside so that I can enter the universe inside my self — and all else that is of importance to me.

The tank has been refined, simplified and made more economical, with much of the refinement done by the Samadhi Tank Company in Santa Monica, California. Together we designed several different kinds of tanks — simple, safe, economical or elaborate, multipurpose, inexpensive.

All my scientific work on dolphins and my books on humans were derived from my work in the tank. The tank is a versatile, multipurpose tool that can aid in bringing further advancement to the human species.

You can learn more about the isolation tank and how to use it for self-exploration in my books, *The Deep Self* and *The Quiet Center.*

SAMADHI TANK

HIGH INDIFFERENCE

I have explored these far-out spaces myself. I have gone into belief systems where I have lived them out for hours, days and weeks. After living in these beliefs and the experiences consequent upon them, then retired from each of the systems, contemplated the results in myself and in those around me, in my changed view of external reality.

Theatre of Selves

When we construct beliefs and live them out, we setup a play within a theater in which we are the author, the composer, the director, the actor and the audience. This capacity of the rather large human brain is to be respected. Its complex capability of the human brain should be understood as we step a side to look its performance in the actual flesh, then we can arrive at a pretty secure foundation within ourselves.

We are essentially alone and our contacts with and feedbacks from others are through rather limited channels — channels prejudiced by our own beliefs and

WE ARE ALONE. OUR CONTACTS WITH AND FEED-BACKS FROM OTH-ERS ARE THROUGH RATHER LIMITED CHANNELS—CHAN-NELS PREJUDICED BY OUR OWN BE-LIEFS AND BY THE BELIEFS OF THOSE WITH WHOM WE COMMUNICATE.

by the beliefs of those with whom we communicate. We can eliminate fear, guilt, and all the other negative aspects of existence. We can also eliminate all the positive aspects of existence and finally arrive at the state of "High Indifference."

High Indifference

When a structure recognizes its own structure, it can become conscious in a way that was not possible before it was aware it was a structure. A computer that can think in terms of its own software and hardware has reached the boundary between software and hardware and can begin to see that pure consciousness is a state of High Indifference. It will not take sides, punish, or reward; it will be totally neutral. Neutral is where it is at.

The state of high computational indifference is amazing. We are the neutral observer, the neutral operator in a biocomputer who does not care about reward or punishment, who cares only about achieving neutral. In this state we can become ecstatic, logically, rationally ecstatic; we can become angry, logically, rationally angry; we can become sexually aroused, logically, rationally sexually aroused, and so on, all within the confines of total computation and rationality. This state is the next level of evolution of that organism from which I speak as a so-called Homo Sapien.

The state of High Indifference is a neutral state, neither punishing nor rewarding. It is a state of understanding, of knowledge or jnana-yoga, beyond ananda, beyond bliss, a state far removed from the trivial primitive compassion of the usual sentimentality given in standard religions. If we pay close attention to our performances we find that the neutral state is actually the most rewarding state we can achieve. It is the state of total objectivity. It is the state of the objective observer, including the objective observer observing itself as a very peculiar system of consciousness and of energies functioning according to laws that we are yet to understand.

We are surrounded with mystery within our own structure, body, or essence. In this state, all or any of these are seeking understanding and some way of avoiding, obliterating or rewriting past misunderstanding. We observe what I have described here as the activity most valued by those in this state.

> The word "Indifference" is not altogether satisfactory but I know of no other that serves as well. It is not at all indifference in the negative or tamasic sense. The latter is a dull, passive, and inert quality, close to the suddenness of real Death. The High Indifference is to be taken in the sense of an utter Fullness that is even more than a bare Infinity. To borrow a figure from mathematics, it is Infinity of some higher order, that is, an INFINITY that comprehends lesser Infinities.
>
> **—MERRELL-WOLFF**

Many have experienced feelings or states similar to those described by Merrell-Wolff. For example, one subject reported that he had gone through an experience in which his feeling of having an eternal existence as being "true" was overwhelming to him. After he passed out of that state of consciousness into his normal, everyday state, he became skeptical of that feeling and of that state of eternal being.

THE NEUTRAL STATE IS THE MOST REWARDING STATE WE CAN ACHIEVE. IT IS THE STATE OF THE OBJECTIVE OBSERVER, INCLUDING THE OBJECTIVE OBSERVER OBSERVING ITSELF. This seems to be a more common occurrence than most people realize. The setting aside of one state of consciousness in another state of consciousness, and calling the second state of consciousness "unreal," "fantastic imaginative," or "self-programmed," is the usual course in our lives.

If states of consciousness are self-programmed, then the basic question arises: Which one of the states of consciousness is independent of the self-programmatic power of the individual? Is there any state of consciousness that is not self-programmed?

To escape answering these questions we appeal to others, to the consensus judgment about reality. And we say: "If I cannot trust my own judgment of the reality of a given state of consciousness, then I must trust the judgment of others whom I designate as "experts" in these matters — priests, psychiatrists, doctors, lawyers, politicians, statesmen, legislators, and so forth. We tend to fall back upon "expert opinion," "expert judgments," in order to escape the necessity of investigating the truth of our own grasp of a given state of consciousness, of a given reality, of a given self-metaprogram.

When we don't share a belief system and a set of experiences having to do with that belief system with a given individual, we tend to put down that individual's belief system and set of experiences as "false," "fantastic imaginary," "self-created," "psychotic," or whatever. This program keeps recurring, in my own experience and that of the most experiences of my colleagues.

THE OBSERVER

Let us assume that I am capable of entering different states of consciousness. Let us number these states of consciousness in an arbitrary way as $state_1$, $state_2$, and so forth to $state_n$. Some of these states are completely separate from one another, some overlap others, and some seem to be identical in the sense that the observer's attitude in the given state is the only change in the variables; that is, I can be in the consensus reality but my observer may take various attitudes or belief systems toward that consensus reality, or any other state other than the consensus reality.

Thus, for heuristic purposes we surround the observer with the elements and the parameters of his state of consciousness as if he were a central sphere, which I call the "observer", surrounded by another sphere, which I call the "state of consciousness."

The observer can be independently changed, as can the state of our consciousness. Each of these may be more or less connected to the external reality, which we will symbolize as a further sphere surrounding the state-

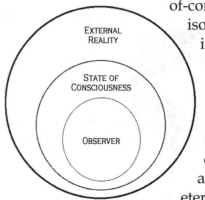

of-consciousness sphere. In isolation this latter sphere is attenuated to the point where it is unimportant and we have only the two inner spheres: that of the self or the observer and the state of consciousness. Here we assume that the parameters of the state of consciousness and its contents can be designated and that the contents of the observer and his or her parameters also can be designated.

In the older terminology the self-metaprogrammer is the central sphere, and the metaprogrammatic space is the next sphere out. For the purposes of experiment, assume that the external reality with its programming is attenuated by solitude, isolation and confinement or by the efforts of the observer in cutting off the external reality, such as is done with a hypnotic trance.

The observer now has many options. We can self-metaprogram the observer and its state; we can also self-metaprogram the state of consciousness, that is, that of the metaprogrammatic space available to us which we are going to bring into our awareness.

If we program in an eternal space, without a body, without this planet, the self-metaprogrammer will become a point within a continuum that contains other points of consciousness, similar to, greater than or less than the observer itself.

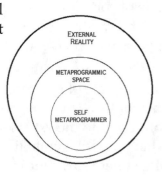

The parameters of this state of consciousness are

> that communication takes place between these point entities,
>
> that they program one another,
>
> that they necessarily be human entities,
>
> that they exist in a universe, which is not referable to the physical universe in our everyday experience.

In this space, there is no knowledge whatsoever that a body exists, that a brain exists, that an individual exists on a planet Earth in a solar system in a galaxy in a universe, such as is described by science as we know it.

We Are Eternal

During the time that the observer is in this space, we feel eternal — that we have no beginning, that we will have no end, and that the other entities with which we are sharing this space are the same as us in this sense. We can receive new information and we can as requested give information to the other entities. This information concerns eternal factors of a network of such beings and their influences on one another. There is no matter in this universe — there are only communicational energies. There is light but light not as we know it through perception by our eyes. There is light that contains the blessed state, the grace of God, the baraka, or whatever other symbol you wish to use to explain this kind of light.

FAIR WITNESS

The crowd in me can become Me, organized into a better business, a better me.

> The Me, administering them, must somehow

respect, admire, love each one but first know each. This
new Me is to become Fair Witness to the rest. Not
judge, not jury, not missionary, not saint-sinner, not
scientist system-researched, not child afraid.

Fair Witness watches and waits. Fair Witness
records, tries to recall exactly. Fair Witness reports
to Me what I do, have done, think, feel, thought, felt.

FAIR WITNESS Fair Witness gives uncontaminated
WATCHES AND testimony, clear bright knowing,
WAITS. unprejudging, noncensoring
observations. Discomfort, pain, fear
from hearing the clean bright truth? To be fair to the
Fair Witness requires me to be the Fair Witness, with no
negativity-positivity, just being.

Self-Metaprogrammer

A basic postulate of the biocomputer view is
that we live within a metaprogrammatic space which
is self-constructed. Everything I do is a metaprogram
in which my biocomputer creates the experience. I
am in my body in a consensus reality, talking to other
entities who are also in bodies, reading books and
exchanging information in the planet-side trip. I speak
from the state in which I am communicating with
other bodies, brains, people. I am not speaking from
the state given above.

Supraself-Metaprogramming

When the self-metaprogrammer is
integrated, when it has become a unitized individual
control system within a given biocomputer, it can
begin to recognize those portions of the programmatic
space, of the simulation space, that may be called
"supraself-metaprogramming." A well-developed,

strong, integrated self-metaprogrammer has options
with regard to supraself-metaprogramming.

Supraself

We enjoy a degree of voluntariness, of decision
making, which was not ours before we became integrated into a single control system. Before we became
a single control system there were several control
systems scattered
through the bio-
computer, any one
of which could take
control and run the
show, without any
necessity for the

ABOUT MY SCHOOL LESSONS, MY FATHER OFTEN ASKED IF I'D LEARNED TO BELIEVE OR TO THINK.

—RALPH NADER

knowledge or cooperation of the others. These control
systems somehow or other must be made aware of
one another and, finally, made into obedient executives under a single administrator that we are calling
the "self-metaprogrammer".

Each biocomputer can develop in such a way as to
reveal these sets of instructions to the supraself. Their
sources seem to be other humans — intuitive, unconscious sources — and some sources which look like
communications networks of civilizations far more
advanced than our current world.

Part of the integration and unification process
that takes place in a given biocomputer is that which
redistributes the hierarchy of priority-listing of
metaprograms. If I have a hierarchy that says, "I, the
self-metaprogrammer, am the most important object
in the universe" then, naturally, nothing is there to
control that self-metaprogrammer. This is a childish
point of view in the sense that the external reality does
not necessarily agree with this point of view; other

persons in the external reality are going to disagree
violently and claim that they are the center of the
universe. This childlike game finally has to terminate
in order to allow mutual survival and mutual progress
on our planet. Wars seem to originate from this kind
of point of view and from a placing of ourselves above
others, from saying that we are superior in making
decisions that have to do with our planet-side trip.

The mature, educated, integrated, unitized self-
metaprogrammer makes certain concessions both
within the external reality and within the inner reality in regard to our ability to control, to evolve, and
to make decisions. The mature self-metaprogrammer
recognizes that there are supraself-metaprograms that
we had best pay close attention to and adopt. These
supraself-metaprograms are guides for decisions to be
made. They are, as it were, handbooks of instructions
on how to live successfully with love and with high
positive energy in the higher states of consciousness.

TAPE LOOPS & TRANSFERENCE

Perhaps you have had sibling-parent situations in the past in which one of the siblings or one of the parents died, leaving the business unfinished. These processes continue automatically below your level of awareness and generate motivations for increasing your intensity of experience with others to resolve problems set up by the tape loops. A tape loop occurs when a loop of tape in a tape reproducer repeats a message again and again.

The young biocomputer in fear, terror, panic, guilt, and so forth, tends to put in overriding orders or instructions for the future operation of that biocomputer as if the current situation were going to be eternal. These instructions remain prominent in the hierarchy in the priority list of instructions for the biocomputer. These are especially powerful in regard to those humans whom we loved as a very young person. We tend to carry

A TAPE LOOP OCCURS WHEN A LOOP OF TAPE IN A TAPE REPRODUCER REPEATS A MESSAGE AGAIN AND AGAIN. these programs forward as if they were still true in an external reality that does not recognize their truth and from which opportunities for actual demonstration of their truth are lacking.

For example, "I am two years old. I am being weaned. My younger brother was just born and he has taken over Mother from me. She is now suckling him and has suddenly stopped suckling me." This unconscious program leads to rage in the young person against the younger brother, but as aging takes place the younger brother can become any other male, and the mother can become any other female with whom the adult becomes interlocked in a love relationship.

A perpetual tendency to try to restore the love relationship between the baby and the mother becomes a tape loop that continues in the adult in inappropriate ways in very uncomfortable triangular situations. The male, for example, attempts to separate a male and a female in order to regain his former pre-eminence with a female—a pre-eminence he does not now have in the external reality but had only with the original mother.

Awareness of such a tape loop does not guarantee that it will cease to have importance in the hierarchy of instructions to the biocomputer. A thorough analysis of it to see how it operates in multiple situations is necessary before the charge can be taken from it and it can be moved down lower in the hierarchical list.

I AM NOT THE TAPE LOOPING

Why do I "give seminars-workshops"?

Is this my new disguise for ego tripping?

Just a more sneaky route to missionary ways?

Who am I?

Real I, existing in front of an audience only?

You, my audience, make real, me.

Without you I am merely a shitful computer unable to love.

To love me, love you, I need you, my audience.

Who am I?

I put myself down this way.

But do I?

Am I not, in writing this, for you, re-entering the same old
     tape-loop, "me and my audience"?

Round and round rotating unhappily

Looping you looping me into the old dance.

This old tape is whirling its senseless self in my computer.

Can it be broken, erased, drowned, removed?

Take out its rotational energy, slow it down.

Watch it play back, Witness.

Know its contents.

On its emoting control track, see, feel the negative-positive swings.

Re-record on this track, dampening the swing peaks.

Play back again, dampen further.

Till finally the Witness is not the tape, the tape not the Witness.

Groovy trip, re-taping emoting loops.

I am not the tapes looping.

Transference Loops

The psychoanalytic name for carrying over unfinished love business from infancy and youth into adulthood is called "transference". Transference is the expression of love or of hatred. It can be either positive or negative for an individual or object on the basis of specific programming from infancy and childhood. Transference can involve a teacher, guru, mate, brother, sister, acquaintance, boss, employee, or whomever.

In the transference relationship the object can detect the positive and the negative aspects of the relationship and, if only insightful, can realize the inappropriateness of the required relationship. About the set of instructions you get from below-levels-of-awareness programming you may say, "This is inappropriate at the present time. It looks as though it may be some historical episode generating these instructions."

Reproductive Programming

The drive to reproduce is a very basic programming in the human animal. It exists in its female form and in its male form. Directly and simply, the young human female wants her uterus filled, and the young human male wants to fill her uterus. This set of species-survival programs is so basic that it is difficult for the young to detect. Only as we strive to detect this set of programs, to put them in perspective, to analyze and look at them with knowledge of transference phenomena, only then can we see their inappropriateness for our supraself-metaprogramming. We produce children almost unconscious of why we are producing them. It is an automatic, hard-wired program and not necessarily reflective of our personal wishes. In a sense, then, the reproductive urges are supraself when we are young, and only with more and more awareness can they possibly become conscious. In most people consciousness of the reproductive urges increases with the increase of distance from the extreme energy that they had when young.

Sexual Scripts

I find that my vehicle is also subject to various kinds of sexual scripts. If I see an attractive blonde, all sorts of sexual movies about the young woman and myself go through my head. Where do these come from? It is absolutely ridiculous that an old man like myself should look at a girl of perhaps twenty and automatically switch on such a sexual movie. It is with a sense of wry humor that I realize this aspect of my ridiculous humanity. Somewhat similarly, if I do not satisfy my sexual urges with my soul mate, a lot of racket having to do with females and males in the everlasting, simple-minded games we play together takes over my computer. It seems to me that the wheel of life is turned by sexual attraction. Let me explain this in more detail.

BEYOND "REPRODUCE!"
SUPRASELF DYAD

We, in this dyad, each have already reproduced.

You have children made, as have I, each with another, not us.

You can no longer become pregnant.

With you I cannot impregnate.

We can love, fuck, ecstatic union.

After many such, what then?

Are we here for sensation's sake?

Can we go beyond, through us and sex?

Where is "beyond"?

Far out spaces, greater beings-entities than us, beckon and call.

Together can we go to them, or is it each of us alone?

Let us try, together, to so go.

Let us face our hindrances, evasions, blocks, and soar, together.

The hindrance of body ecstasy tied here convert to spirit travel energy there.

The hindrance of planet earth, mother ties to her bosom, use constructively.

The evasion of loss of independent self, convert to dyad greatness.

Together fusing into one to travel as two-in-one.

No rivalry, no control for each separate over other, one directed by each of two, fused.

A dream, a fantasy? Poetry?

No.

A program, a metaprogram for a Supraself dyad.

I sever, I distinguish, I cross, I call, I name.

The universe of confusion is mapped, navigated, I pilot myself through it.

A pilot, a navigator, an engine appear, for the engine an engineer

The I-Me spaces distinguish and sever themselves into

"I pilot, I navigate, I furnish the energy, the engine.

I move, I cross, I map, I name, I call.

So Inner Universes I can explore.

Now I can communicate with you."

As we age, we tend to divert energy away from this system into other systems of thought, feeling and doing. The original energy is incredible in its power and its quantity. Only with time does its urgency diminish. Numbers of trips around the sun are necessary before the realization of how powerful and how unconscious this system of programs really is. It is almost as if until we have fulfilled our reproduction instructions and produced one, or two, or more children, the force of these programs will not diminish. It is as if we have to have children in order never to have to have children again.

Our children can teach us a good deal of truth about our past history. To a certain extent we can see in miniature, as it were, that which we had to go through. We can also see that it is almost impossible to communicate our accrued wisdom to the younger generation as we live with them. Their selective forgetting, their selective awareness, are so obvious to older people, even as, to the young, the lack of certain energies in older adults is obvious.

REPROGRAMMING METABELIEFS

Metabeliefs are being programmed and reprogrammed all the time, without our being aware of it. Certain altered states of consciousness facilitate purposeful programming. In modern Western life we tend toward using alcohol, drugs and tobacco to change from one mental state into another. Most mind-states achieved through these chemicals are mind-numbing rather than mind-expanding. However, one class of drugs known as "entheogens" alters the mind in such a way as to render it hyper-programmable.

Reprogramming Power

Basic beliefs can be unearthed – possibly even changed – during the entheogenic experience, which is desirable and at the same time perilous. The temptation to elicit, to control, and to change the beliefs of others and one's own can be a seductive goal.

Entheogens put reprogramming power in the hands of those who use them. But there is danger that entheogens can promote self-deluding beliefs.

Powerful entheogens allow us to take ours lives apart, as it were, and to look at separate areas of belief independently of beliefs about those areas, that is, independently of our metabeliefs. For example, if you believe, even temporarily, that you are a god when in the entheogenic state, you *become* a god in your imagination. You become your concept of God in terms of how powerful, how omniscient, how knowledgeable a god you can be. When in the entheogenic state we are no longer influenced by the usual metabelief, "I am in a class of animals known as Homo Sapiens, not in a class above the animal class known as gods".

When in the entheogenic state we can ignore what we know in one area and construct a belief about another area contradicting the first and have freedom to carry out many of the logical consequences regardless of how irrational or how out of step the belief is with reality or with our other belief systems. In this sense entheogens can be thought of as facilitating the genesis of psychosis itself rather than mimicking of psychosis.

Beliefs About Mind-Altering

The ability to hold a very powerful, non-rational belief in mind and act as if it is true within your own mind is one aspect of psychosis. If and when an entheogenic state or similar state persists beyond the expected limits of six to ten hours of usual influence, then we begin to suspect that other biochemical and neurological mech-

ENTHEOGENS PUT REPROGRAMMING POWER IN THE HANDS OF THOSE WHO USE THEM.

anisms are activated which might possibly be similar, if not identical, to those occurring during "true psychosis."

Psychotomimetic

LSD was called "psychotomimetic" quite early in the analysis of its effects, which created a history of it as a "psychotomimetic drug." This judgment acts as a programming agent for all subsequent work with LSD. This is embedded in the literature, it is embedded in the guiding agencies for its investigation, it is embedded in the public mind and wherever we turn we are faced with this tradition of "psychotomimesis."

I recall a rather amusing story with respect to this view of the perils of LSD, an exceptionally powerful entheogen. A well-known psychiatrist was approached by a woman who had read his work on LSD and was worried about what LSD might do to her mind and brain. When she questioned him, he answered, "I have written that LSD causes psychosis and I am sure that it does for a period of at least four to eight hours." She asked, "And what do you mean by 'psychosis'?" At that

BASIC BELIEFS CAN BE UNEARTHERD AND CHANGED DURING THE ENTHEOGENIC EXPERIENCE.

point the psychiatrist's wife interrupted and said, "Let me tell you a little story which will illustrate what he means by the word 'psychosis.'

One night he came home from the laboratory complaining that he was getting some sort of virus disease. I asked him to describe his symptoms in detail. As he began to describe the symptoms it suddenly occurred to him that these were the symptoms of the LSD state. He then thought back during the day and discovered that by accident be had apparently absorbed some LSD in the course of his experiments earlier that day. At this point he said, 'Oh, it's just an LSD psychosis. I am going to bed and sleep it off,' which he did."

This story illustrates what a strong-minded, self-disciplined and responsible individual thinks about the effects of LSD on himself. There are weaker individuals who are precipitated into a "real," difficult-to-reverse psychosis by the drug experience. Some people who are thusly susceptible and must be cautious about using entheogens.

Religious Awakening

Another widespread belief surrounding the use of entheogens is that it stimulates a "religious revelation". This belief has done as much of a disservice to our understanding of what is going on as has the "psychotomimesis" belief. We cannot take responsibility for "religious transcendental experiences" scientifically. Psychosis mimicking and religious experiences are a little bit beyond the reach of proper scientific investigation.

WORRY OVER UNEXPLAINED EXPERIENCES CAN BE QUELLED WHEN THOSE EXPERIENCES FIT INTO ESTABLISHED BELIEFS.

So without any empirical basis we generally accept the belief that entheogens like LSD mimic psychosis and can cause religious transcendental experiences. These points of view have been supported by innumerable books describing personal experiences under LSD, such as those by Jane Dunlap, Constance Newland, M. C. Bishop, Aldous Huxley, Timothy Leary, Richard Alpert and Ralph Metzner.

If entheogenic effects could be fully accounted for by these beliefs, the scientific work would not be as difficult as it is. If we could only go along with these "wishful thinking" views of the effects, if we could go along with those who saw only these things when they took the entheogenic substance, then our work would not be very difficult. We could agree that the explanations were adequate and we could drop the whole subject. But these explanations are scientifically unsatisfactory because they have led to "mental absolutes" which seem to me to be unreasonable. Basically these accounts are expressions of wishful thinking by the authors. I do not say that this is irresponsible reportage of inner events. These people are sincere, straightforward, and disciplined along their own lines. However, they have given us that which they wish to be true, rather than what has been demonstrated empirically to be true.

In my view, this literature can be summarized by saying that these elaborate constructs reflect two things from the authors. First, the contents of their own memory has been recombined in a free associational way, and second, it is the realization of their most secret and hoped-for set of goals with regard to their own basic beliefs, in so far as these could be accomplished within their heads

Seductive

The social effects of these sorts of writings include a rather devastating seduction of young minds toward the taking of entheogens. The promise of "ecstasy" and "religious transcendence" to some of the youngsters is very seductive. To others the promise of "psychotic experience" is equally seductive. Let us not forget that adventure beckons to the young

and that the frontier of the mind has been opened up by such entheogenic substances for the perusal of those seeking adventure, both for pleasure and for danger.

A subculture has built up around these substances. Large numbers of students have read such writings and established a peer mythology with regard to these writings. From my discussions with several of these youngsters I was left with the impression that the motives involved are quite complex and worthy of a good deal of further study. In the light of this kind of experience, it is high time that we instituted a thorough and spread scientific investigation of what is going on among these youngster's use of entheogens.

Scientific Approach Needed

Let us try to arrive at objective and scientific views of the effect of entheogens upon the mind. This is indeed not easy but I believe that it is important to try. The objective, dispassionate, and thorough investigation of states of mind induced by entheogenic substances is a primary requirement for science for the next few years. We cannot eliminate the subjective report as a source of data. We should not allow subjective reportage to become merely an artistic and romantic medium for use only by novelists and artists. The science of a mentality as reported by that mentality has been neglected in academic science because it is considered anecdotal. The increase in cognitive psychology is encouraging and to be applauded and, hopefully, expanded.

The subjective aspects of mental functioning in adolescence is incredibly important to the self. Many young people seek guidance, seek help and seek education in this world of the subjective and do not obtain much help from science. The only maps of the territories they have are those of the artists, theologians, and psychiatrists who preceded them in the entheogenic state. It is my view that young people need a catalog of possible maps and an estimate of the probabilities of the occurrence of certain kinds of maps in this area, and maps of the dead ends and lethal traps.

To construct a set of ideas which may be of help in educating the young in regard to the inner life with special reference to entheogenic states, there must be an understanding that the "creatures seen, felt, heard," and the "beings thought to and thought from" when under the influence of a powerful entheogen are constructs of our mind drawn from our imagination and of the elements stored within us. From the multitude of materials in our memory, we can construct through imagination any conceivable living breathing kind of creature. We can construct thinking machines or thinking beings or other people with any desired set of characteristics and any desired set of powers, within the limits of our conceptions.

Caution

The entheogenic state differs from ordinary dreaming, ordinary daydreaming, and wishful thinking in general in the greater brilliance and the greater intensity of the projected visual images and in the greater intensity of the feelings aroused, coupled with these images, sights, and sounds. It is as if the entheogen puts a noisy amplifier in your computer, an amplifier of the emotive and cognitive processes of your mind. This noisy amplifier gives the subjective impression of increased powers of control over our thinking processes. This is a false impression caused by the energy of the added random noise. We may not

USING "IMAGINATION," WE CAN CONSTRUCT ANY CONCEIVABLE LIVING, BREATHING KIND OF CREATURE FROM THE MULTITUDE OF MATERIALS IN OUR MEMORY. have such control but we have the impression that we do. This effect under the influence of a powerful entheogen may be caused by the forced turning inward of our self, away from a less interesting external reality and paying more attention to our highly active inner processes excited by the noise. A primary effect seems to be as if rewarding brain systems are stimulated and the punishing systems inhibited.

The important cautions, then, are that entheogens have a seductive history, and cause states of mind that are so seductive that subjects want to return for further experiences. Importantly, subjects are open to influence and are very vulnerable in this state. They become very programmable by other persons. They are quite at the command of their own pleasurable desires and their own wishful thinking in greater measure than is comfortable to contemplate.

Long-term subtle psychological damage may result; such damage may long be hidden by the pleasure and enthusiasm engendered by the substance. It is possible that in long-term use, brains are structurally damaged. Thus subjects may be weakened by this substance attacking them literally where they live.

Subjects are being seduced by a chemical rewarding of mental life without working for the reward. The new stimuli for the new lotus-eaters are subtle and subtly evasive, hiding insight itself under unearned chemical rewards given for free.

Educate for Responsibility

Is education for responsibility possible
with the use of such chemicals? I do not know. I am interested, and am trying to understand. Who has taken
responsibility? No one — so far. A fantasy of attaining a
goal, a mental imagining of achieving a goal, fully bio-
chemically rewarded, may become a fixed belief, a way
of life. I don't like the feel of it. It is wrong, somehow.

If states of consciousness are self-programmed,
then the basic question arises: Which one of the states
of consciousness is independent of the self-programmatic power of the individual? Is there any state of
consciousness which is not self-programmed?

To escape answering these questions we appeal to
others, to the consensus judgment about reality. And
we say: "If I cannot trust my own judgment of the
reality of a given state of consciousness, then I must
trust the judgment of others whom I designate as
'experts' in these matters" — priests, psychiatrists, doctors, lawyers, politicians, statesmen, legislators, and
so forth. One tends to fall back upon "expert opinion,"
"expert judgment."

There are well-established, acceptable, social ways
of changing consciousness. In my belief system, non-
chemical ways of changing consciousness should be
taught to youngsters so that they can master them
while they are still young enough to be sufficiently
flexible to change their programming. The alternatives to drugs as steersman have been around a long
time and should be explored in great depth within our
culture. With the new imports of teachers from Tibet,
from Japan, from China, many of these techniques are
entering into our culture. The alternative belief systems
of the esoteric schools for obtaining altered states of
consciousness are very ancient and well-established.

Evasions of Responsibility

The number of young persons experimenting with LSD brings in its wake many of the older problems faced by parents and educators in regard to the development of those factors that we epitomize in the word "responsibility".

Others have experienced feelings or states similar to those described by Merrell-Wolff. For example, one subject reported that he had just gone through an experience in which his feeling of having an eternal existence as being "true" was overwhelming to him. After he passed out of that state of consciousness into his normal, everyday state, he became skeptical of that feeling and of that state of eternal being.

This seems to be a more common occurrence than most people are aware of. The setting aside of one state of consciousness in another state of consciousness, and calling the second state of consciousness "unreal," "fantastic," "imaginative," or "self-programmed," is the usual course in such cases.

In the matrix of our civilization each one of us has multiple exchanges and responsibilities for many different aspects of that civilization. The basis of responsibility and its education is found in the basic structure of the feeling-thinking machinery of the individual. One view of responsibility is that of an inner discipline which directs the activities of the self toward attainable and idealistic goals. These goals may be directed so as to be strictly personal or they may be directed for others than one's self. The goals may be connected with only a few persons or large numbers of persons

Each of us has a more or less fluid reference point within the structure of society. We are regulated in detail by taxation, by income, by available work, by

husband, by wife, by children, by parents, by governments, large and small. Each of these separate agents
and agencies exacts its toll of time, effort, and money
from us. Each agent and agency has ways of enforc-
ing its toll upon each one of us in the absence of a
response and continuing responsibility from each one
of us toward each one of them.

As we grow from the non-speaking little animal
born into this world to responsible adults with our
own families, we are required to expand our responsibility to the outside world again and again. Only
when responsible people judge us to be unfit to accept
further responsibility does the pressure to expand the
areas of our responsibility decrease. Irrespective of our
individual desires, this inexorable process continues
throughout out lives.

Inside each of us is an answer to these external
calls to duty. At each stage we test the system to discover its limits and how to respond with appropriate
action, thinking, and dedication. At each young stage
the various kinds of evasions of responsibility are
tried to the limits possible to us as a person and rejected or further espoused, depending upon the inner
satisfaction generated by the evasive action.

The evasions for the young usually take the form
of pursuing the most pleasurable paths and staying
away from those that are found to be unpleasant or
painful. However, as we grow older and more experienced, the pleasure and pain become more than
physiological experiences and have begun to attach
themselves to concepts, to persons, to institutions, to
real things, and to distant goals. When our brains have
enlarged enough and become experienced enough in
controlling the algebraic sign (plus or minus) of the
emotional value of various systems of thinking and

successes within those systems, the basic structure
for responsibility has been achieved. The responsible,
strong self-directed individual with dedication and
interest in improvement of self and one's area of responsibility is the person to keep in mind in the rest of
this discussion.

Who is Responsible?

Let us look at a distribution curve of responsible
persons. At one end are those of minimal responsibility and at the other are end those of maximal responsibility. This curve of the number of people with each
degree of responsibility varies with quite a large number of parameters. It varies with age, with economic
level, and with educational level achieved. Some
of these individuals are selected by the educational
system for the very factor that we are discussing: that
is, the more responsible individuals with intelligence
will either continue their education and complete it or
will have found what they are looking for outside this
system of education and have accepted responsible
jobs on which they start their life's work.

As John Gardner says in his book *Excellence*, that
there is no *a priori* reason that all those with intelligence, responsibility, and dedication should pass
through the college system. There are other means
of reaching social and national responsible positions
than through college. Gardner points out that we have
people on arbitrary scales of value, placing those who
have loafed their way through college higher than
those who have achieved in large measure through a
self-education regime. The latter makes a more valuable person than the former.

All of these considerations are relevant to the popularity of entheogens. The bad press having to do with college students taking psychedelics, the controls of the Federal Food and Drug Administration and the National Institute of Mental Health underscore this problem. One might ask: Who is responsible with regard to these powerful mind-altering substances? Where lies the responsibility for educating for responsibility with regard to using them?

This is a difficult problem. In my opinion the abdication of responsibility for entheogens started in the early 1950s when certain people began to take these substances and report their experiences in the scientific and nonscientific literature. Using the "20/20 vision of hindsight," let us reconstruct what seems to have happened.

First of all the effects of these substances have been known for a long time. Naturally occurring plants and fungi which are the biochemical factories for these substances have been around literally millions of years. Man has incorporated some of these into past religious rites and certain "pagan" groups have used them with telling effect in their religious rituals. In so far as we can discover, each of these groups has had to face the problem of discipline with regard to the use of these substances. A cogent example of the achievement of discipline in order to control the use of these substances is the Native American Church, with the peyote cactus. The history of this group has been recounted many times. From the published accounts we can deduce that responsible use was achieved within the confines of a religious setting. In *Sacred Mushrooms of the Goddess: The Secrets of Eleusis,* classics professor Carl Ruck presents an in depth discussion of the ancients' ritual use of entheogens.

It may be that responsible use of these substances cannot be achieved without some sort of strictures in the direction of the religious aspects. A religious transformation of the individual may be a step on the way toward achievement of inner responsibility to himself. Let us move from the religious viewpoint to a more basic philosophical viewpoint in which we explore the basic beliefs that we have and on which we actually operate. In this context we will try to ignore the tendency of most persons to say that they believe certain things, whereas in reality they act as if they believe quite something else. In this context we are speaking of only those basic beliefs which are operationally, demonstratively existent in the behavior and in the accomplishments of the individual.

HIGHER CONSCIOUSNESS
THROUGH CHEMISTRY

An intimate connection exists between us in this brain and the chemistry of that brain. If we can change the molecular configuration of the brain by injecting suitable substances into the bloodstream or into muscles, then there must be some very intimate connection between us in this brain and the state of the chemistry of that brain. To some persons this is a "drag." What? I'm the victim of chemistry? The answer lies not in deprecating or resenting this fact; it lies in exploring this fact and finding out what kinds of molecules are absolutely essential to our existence and what kinds disturb the homeostasis that we want we seek.

Some people are quite content with maintaining a range of molecular configurations in their brains through proper foods, exercise, sleep, work and play. These people get their adventure from skiing, skydiving or whatever. They allow the play of the body itself to change the chemistry of the brain and thus to change their states of consciousness.

Chemical Tools

The majority of the Eastern gurus
recommend the cessation of the use of drugs, feeling
that the old-fashioned methods of changing our state
of consciousness by exercises, inner discipline and
boredom, and by solitude, isolation and confinement,
are far better. After approximately twenty-five years
of experimentation with each of these methods, I came
to the same conclusion. It is far better to use consistent
daily exercises—mental, physical and spiritual—than
it is to use drugs.

I rather resent the fact that when I take a drug, I
have signed a contract with a chemical for the specific period of time that it exerts powerful influences
upon everything I do, think, feel, or am. Then the
effect wears off, leaving me in a state of wonderment
that such a small quantum of a substance could so
profoundly affect my being. It was after I had experimented with Ketamine that I saw LSD, Ketamine,
and various other chemicals that change my thinking,
feeling, being, and doing as merely small tools in a
much larger context. They are not the psychotomimetic or psychosis producing, or horror brainwashing
substances that the press taught us to believe they are.
They are merely chemical tools useful in the proper
context for those who are exploring the human brain
and the human mind and the possible parameters and
variations of its states of being.

Access to the Gods

Certain tribes in Mexico accept as desirable the taking of sacred mushrooms or peyote with social rituals, beliefs, and control by the elders of the tribe. The
Indians revere the changes in states of being, states

of consciousness, induced by psilocybin mushrooms, peyote, and other substances. They pursue these states in order to control their gods to a certain extent and propitiate them behind the phenomena of the universe. They believe they converse with and influence their rain gods and fertility gods when under the influence of these substances.

I was rather amused when my son, John, went into these cultures and was fed stories that very much resembled stories Don Juan told Carlos Castaneda in *The Teachings of Don Juan*. John found that the shamans—apparently Don Juan was one of these—will do anything they can to satisfy an investigator from America. They concoct fantasies, stories, anything to satisfy the investigator, thus protecting themselves from encroachment by the foreigner's belief systems.

The people I am speaking of are isolated Indian groups. For example, the Toapuri culture is a pure peyote one. This group had not been wholly over taken by Christian beliefs and have maintained nearly pure Aztec religion, although they have increasingly given in to using mechanical devices as our machine civilization has encroached upon them,

The Toapuri's navigation is steered by flexible beliefs that are used as a way of thinking out difficult problems when all the information necessary to solve the problems is not available.

The Toapuri have a marvelous sense of humor. The facile sense of humor these people have is directed toward themselves and the universe around them as well as toward their gods. At the time of the great peyote-taking, which occurs once a year, behavior is allowed which would be punishable in the North by fine or imprisonment. While the sexual mores change during this period, the activity is regulated and car-

ried out according to directions received through the
shamans from the gods they worship.

Programming Tools

There are literally millions of people
who take drugs in the modern Western cultures. Some
are taken on prescription with Establishment approv-
al; others are taken illegally. We label as "drugs" many
substances which scientifically speaking, are actually
"purified chemicals," and generally organic, meaning
that they consist of carbon compounds of one sort or
another. There are also the products of the biological
activities of other organisms, called "biologicals" such
as penicillin. Of the literally thousands of such chemical compounds, only those that in some way change
consciousness concern us here. These "mind drugs"
are of prime importance in the metabelief that drugs
are a reliable guide for navigating one's life.

Concomitant with drugs that change consciousness there is what I call "the program written on the pill-kind of
reasoning". If you are given a pill
that is said to do something to your
body or mind, you then expect the
pill to have certain effects. Such
expectations are "programs".

**WHAT IS
REWARDED
TENDS TO BE
REPEATED.**

Large numbers of youth routinely use the rather
dangerous group of drugs derived from the opium
poppy—morphine, heroin, and so forth. These drugs
are characterized by a double psychopharmacological effect. The first effect is one of dreamy peace, of
contentment that precludes any interest in what is
going on outside oneself, of being on "Cloud Nine"
irrespective of actual circumstances. This initial effect is deeply rewarding. The experience of reward is

the mechanism by which programs are "saved." What is rewarded tends to be repeated. And if the ex- perience of reward comes **THE *EXPERIENCE OF REWARD* IS THE MECHA- NISM BY WHICH PRO- GRAMS ARE "SAVED."** with the action, such as smoking cigarettes, again and again, the programs becomes ever more powerful. Ad- diction begins here. However, addiction is not guar- anteed until the person has to face withdrawal from these chemicals and the pleasing effects they trigger.

At the time of withdrawal there occur very power- ful symptoms: feelings of great restlessness, aches and pains, and in extreme cases, seizure-like activity of the central nervous system. Withdrawal is painful, and re- quires a strong personality to survive it. Such groups as Synanon, Delancy House, and The Bridge attempt to strengthen the personality of addicts in such a way that, with group support, they can go through with- drawal.

Drugs have gotten involved in a large social feed- back system, including very heavy penalties for distri- bution, possession, or the use of these chemicals. The Federal Government has its own agency to control or attempt to control traffic in these drugs. The basic belief system operating this feedback system is that "heroin is addictive for everyone; therefore we must protect everyone from heroin".

Very careful research into this question shows the belief that heroin is all-powerful and capable of de- stroying personalities is true — largely only for those who believe it to be true. It has been demonstrated again and again that addicts have certain kinds of personalities before they start on heroin, personalities that make them susceptible to the addiction program. They can become alcoholics, they can become morphine addicts, they can become addicted to gambling, and so on. There is something basically different about these people. For example, in Spanish Harlem in New York City it was shown that when a group of boys of age sixteen mainlined on heroin, only 3 percent of them became addicted. The rest went through withdrawal with no overpowering temptation to use heroin again.

Addictive drugs have given the Federal Government its lever for controlling substances of other sorts, including the plant *cannabis sativa*, otherwise known as marijuana. Through the efforts of Harry Anslinger, then head of the Federal Bureau of Narcotics, marijuana was labeled as a narcotic in 1937 and placed into the same category as heroin, morphine, and other addictive substances, where it continues to be so categorized. Anslinger's "program written on a weed" was a "panic program". It assumed that marijuana is as dangerous as the derivatives of opium. That was incorporated into law and is still perpetuated.

Since then millions of people have demonstrated that this weed is not addictive, but the lives of many people continue to be ruined because they are jailed for the possession of marijuana. The national program on drugs has brought us to a very peculiar state of divisiveness in which the law defines the reality as one thing, and the direct experience of millions demonstrates quite the opposite.

This situation is remindful of the Volstead Act prohibiting alcohol, which was finally repealed under President Roosevelt in 1933. In 1918, Congressman Andrew J. Volstead and his followers managed to pass the Eighteenth Amendment, forbidding the manufacture, sale and transportation of alcoholic beverages. The law became conspicuous for the absence of compliance among the populace. Millions of Americans in the twenties and thirties who had any money at all had a "friend" who knew a bootlegger who brought alcohol across the border from Canada or Mexico, or across the Atlantic or Pacific oceans.

Fortunes were made and lost on the unlawful sale of alcoholic beverages as drinking attained a popularity far surpassing pre-Prohibition levels. Thousands of people began making wine in their attics and gin in their bathtubs. Hundreds of millions of dollars were spent in attempting to enforce this unrealistic law. A large number—even prominent citizens of the country—were fighting against this dictate of their government, secretively and often recklessly, because of both the poor quality of much of the alcohol and the danger of arrest. Respect for the law was at a low ebb.

Belief: Drugs Are Bad

Drugs are bad as a belief won out as far as the legislators were concerned. Laws were made in a panic about the consequences of taking of these drugs. Few if any of the legislators understood the issues involved, and whenever researchers who best understood the issues attempted to speak up they were discredited, in many cases by their own colleagues. The credibility gap became extreme within the medical profession between those who had taken LSD and those who had not. The enthusiastic proponents of these chemicals tried to oversell them and were fought back by those who were frightened by them. The resulting belief about drugs seems to have resulted from over valuation of the positive benefits of the psychedelics by those who are advocating their use, and the fear of those who had not taken them and who had heard various horror stories about using them.

There was a short period from 1933 to 1937 when we were free of such laws in the United States. Within four years after the Eighteenth Amendment was repealed by the Twenty-First Amendment, the marijuana law was put into effect. The same so-called "do-gooders" were once again in control, creating laws and the agencies to enforce them, carrying on a kind of warfare against a large segment of the population.

Psychopharmacological Effects

Let us look behind these powerful social movements and examine some of the psychopharmacological effects of the drugs, including the psychedelics, that are brought under question. For thousands, if not hundreds of thousands of years, humans have sought to change consciousness through plants and the tinctures and essences derived from plants. In the 19th Century some chemical constituents of these plants that brought about various changes in consciousness were isolated, purified, and made available through mass production.

Cocaine

Peruvian Indians who had to carry heavy loads at high altitudes for long periods of time chew the leaves of the coca plant to ward off fatigue. Coca leaves are not of themselves addictive. As Richard Schultes, the Harvard botanist, showed, Peruvian Indians drafted into the Peruvian Army tossed off the habit without any withdrawal symptoms, for example. In Western society cocaine is not particularly addictive, except for those people who are hard-wired to become addicted to something.

Cocaine was first isolated by Merck & Company in the late 1800s. At the age of twenty-eight Sigmund Freud was pushing the benefits of cocaine, giving it to his fiancée and taking it himself daily. He wrote a brief monograph on the subject, which today reads like that of a psychedelic enthusiast. Freud thought cocaine a cure-all when he experimented with the use of cocaine for breaking the morphine habits of some of his colleagues and for reliev- **COCA LEAVES ARE NOT OF THEMSELVES ADDICTIVE.** ing nervous and mental disorders. Only as he found that someone addicted to morphine readily becomes addicted to cocaine did he realize he was wrong, as in the case of his friend Fliess.

Mescaline

The next powerful chemical iso-lated from a plant was mescaline. Dr. Weir Mitchell of Philadelphia gave us accurate descriptions of its mind-changing qualities, reported in experiments with mescaline in the 1880s. Mescaline is isolated from the peyote cactus and has been used for centuries in the religious rites of various Indian tribes in North America. Many descriptions of its effects are given by Castaneda in his series of books about Don Juan.

Mescaline, which occupied many shelves of many laboratories for several decades, was noticed only by scientists interested in its properties. Not until the psy-chedelic era of the 1960s did it come to be considered a dangerous substance.

LSD

In 1938 Albert Hoffman isolated LSD-25 from the rye fungus—ergot. In 1942 when he took a small dose—about 250 micrograms—he found that it had powerful mind-changing qualities. About that experi-ence he wrote a paper with Stoller in which he said that LSD-25 was psychotomimetic in the sense that it induced a psychosis-like state in those who took it. When LSD-25 was brought to the United States in the 1950s, a program was written on it: "psychotomimetic."

On the fertile soil prepared by the marijuana underground, the distribution of LSD-25 took root and became national. Hundreds of thousands of people took it; some were institutionalized with mental illnesses attributed to having taken the substance. Considering the large number of users, the number of casualties has been small—much smaller, for example, than the annual death rate on the highways. Nonetheless, the public outcry through the media, especially a magazine article in *Life* in 1966, forced legislation against the psychedelics in general and LSD-25 in particular. Laws with heavy penalties were enacted, Federal and State, against the possession, use and sale of these substances.

Belief: Drugs Are Good

In the West we are brought up to believe in doctors as an expert. When the doctor prescribes a pill for an illness, we take it without question. The doctor in this case has the powers of the old priesthood in the sense that we do not have the knowledge to question the doctor's decisions, nor do we want to. Instead we look for the best doctor we can find and we trust him.

This trusting acceptance of drugs prescribed for us by a doctor is a well-established part of our way of life. The first psychologically active agents useful in the control of people were the tranquilizers discovered in the 1950s. Among these were the phenothiazines. It was my impression at the National Institute of Mental Health, and the impression of various psychotherapists who saw these drugs first used at St. Elizabeth's Hospital in Washington, that all these tranquilizers did was remove the possibility that the patient would misbehave. In other words, these were behavioral control chemicals which did not cure anything but merely prevented patients from acting out their fantasies and giving in to fits of rage or other difficult-to-control states as Ken Kesey's *One Flew Over the Cuckoo's Nest* so aptly portrayed.

Tranquilizers

One psychotherapist said that the patients on tranquilizers "looked like lizards asleep in the sun." Yet, he knew that down inside they were still extremely troubled people and that the tranquilization was merely an institutional kind of chemical straitjacket making them easier to manage.

One of the early tranquilizers, derived from a plant from India called Rauwolfia Serpentina marketed in the United States as Serpasil, discharged the biological battery and brought on fatigue to the point where patients, although they remained fully conscious, could not object to anything that happened to them. Since those early days of tranquilizers literally hundreds of such chemicals have been discovered which can induce altered states of consciousness to prevent outbreaks of excitement without sacrificing conscious awareness.

Slowly but surely, the tranquilizers have been accepted by Establishment medicine and put on prescription. Now they are routinely marketed on TV to reduce shyness and anxiety—states believed to be a normal part of life in earlier times. Consensus beliefs evolve. Increasingly, it is believed that we should not suffer even the smallest emotional upset or discomfort—when there is a pharmaceutical available to render us feeling good again.

Amphetamines

The amphetamines were originally thought to be psychic energizers, but it developed that they were merely energizers of lower levels of energy within the biological system. Later, real psychic energizers turned out to be what the medical profession had been hunting for—substances with the ability to induce higher energy in low-energy people without altering their state of consciousness.

Thus the "drugs are good" mythology was extended to tranquilization, to high-energy states, in addition to the old stand-bys such as sleeping pills like barbiturates and so forth. The results were obtained without the penalties that alcohol exacts, such as a bad hangover, liver damage and brain damage. The status of alcohol was re-instated in the Establishment, put under adequate Federal controls, and sold under government auspices in the various states of the United States. Alcohol seems to be the mainstay of most people in the United States who desire to change consciousness a little bit, but not too much.

There are those who cannot get to sleep without barbiturates, who cannot wake up without an amphetamine, and who obtain drugs through legal prescriptions. There are those who cannot function without tranquilizers. These people number in the hundreds of thousands, if not the millions.

There are millions of people who cannot get along without their late afternoon drink, or without their cocktail at lunch. Those who must smoke tobacco to obtain the effects of the various resins and the nicotine in tobacco number in the millions. Withdrawal symptoms from alcohol, from barbiturates, are very severe. When accustomed to a fairly high level of these substances in the blood, withdrawal can, for example, cause convulsions.

PART TWO

METABELIEFS WE STEER BY

GROUP PRESSURE

Human groups and their demands upon us are ever present, day and night, awake and asleep. At times peer pressure permeates our lives almost to the exclusion of everything else. Without being members of groups we would not have language itself; we would not have electricity, automobiles, gas supplies; we would not have telephones, TV, radio; we would not have highways, ships, airplanes; we would not have materials to build our own house; we would not have much of anything.

This incredible dependence of the individual on the group in modern civilization can become stultifying and non-creative. However, once we realize that a certain minimum of this relationship with groups is absolutely necessary for our survival, we can see how willing we are to put up with group activity in order to maintain our standard of living and standard of survival.

Each of us is born into a dyad and completes a triadic relationship. If there are children

born ahead of us, we are born into a family group
that places its demands upon us almost at birth. The
newborn baby is an object of interest to almost everybody and as it grows its upbringing is of interest to
everyone in the family. The seductive aspects of group
activity are here presented to the baby in full panoply.
The sticky love and hate relationships that dominate
our lives are here present in embryo and in full-blown
catastrophe.

TO A BROTHER AND FAMILY

I put myself outside your home, as if a cage. When
young and eager, I knew not joy in cagement. My spirit
called me out of your town, away from home. On my
return thirty-six years later now I know. No rebel I today;
I grieve that warmth solidity. Your home, your children
I love, appreciate as one from outside the walls of love
and humor you built. The law, the profit, and the fiscal
response-ability you all show. It's beautiful. An artistic
creation of long years of loving interaction. I admire
what you do, have done, where you are. I wish, and turn
away from wishful thinking. I cannot rewrite history,
my own, or of others. Much I "could have done, but
did not." Much I "did but regret having done." Much I
"should have done, but did not." Much I did and do not
regret, am glad I did. Where I am I do not know. I am
told now what to do. Someone somewhere, I believe,
now tells me.

I hope they wish me well and do not test me to
destruction.

A baby in a love relationship possesses a whole
universe, which is expanding him and itself. Older
siblings may try to do away with him or to love him to
death. Younger siblings will displace him from mother

and from other members of the group, so he must establish his own relationships—his own group, if you wish. Some children join already-formed groups; others from their own groups. Let us look at these children-groups for a moment.

Children Groups

The strongest members of any group dictate the terms for becoming a member and maintaining membership and also the rules for removing a member from the group. There are initiation rites for joining the group, and rituals for being a continued member, such as contributions in financial support and in work to be performed for the group, for example. There are peer criteria of performance; there are judgments made of each person's individual performance, accomplishments, feelings, and what we say as a member of the group.

There is a continual exchange of gossip among the members. Each group develops its palace politics, which becomes a constant source of new rumors about what is or is not going to happen next in terms of group interest or activities. There are attempts by the leadership to create and have the group create dramatic happenings involving non-members of the group to demonstrate the strength of the group and its superiority to non-members. Secret signs, even a secret language may develop; there are special knocks to open a door, there are special places for meeting, usually hidden. There are careful observations of the behavior of members when they are seated from the group; there are loyalty tests based upon criteria set up by the leadership of the group. There is expectation that the members will praise the leadership for its activities and that the leaders will praise the members for theirs.

All the various mechanisms that Irving L. Janis discusses in *The Victims of Groupthink* are present in children groups. It is out of such young groups that adult "groupthink" models are derived. To a child who is a member of an elite group, say a very active one, which brings a lot of satisfaction, that group becomes all-powerful. Much of children's thinking, feeling, and doing are centered on the group. He feels that he doesn't amount to anything except as a member of the group. The children's individual accomplishments and status lose their meaning, while becoming one of Them.

The concept of transference is demonstrated most strongly in such groups. The child's love, awe, fear and guilt from his original trial are now transferred to an entity known as "The Group". Such a group, if organized by adults and watched over very carefully by adults, can lead these children into casting the group onto the national scene. In the United States we have such "children groups" as the Boy Scouts of America, the Campfire Girls, The Boys and Girls Clubs of America, military schools, all sorts of church groups in the various denominations all perpetuated in such special boys' or girls' clubs as the Elks, the Kiwanis, the Rotary, the Masons, the Rebeccas, the D.A.R., the hierarchy of the Catholic Church; Police Departments; Fire Departments; the United States Army, Air Force, and Navy.

Adult Groups

As we mature we can join any number of groups that are totally organized and will organize our lives for us. There is no need for independent thought, independent feeling, or independent action, if we want to avoid them. If we look to The Group as a navigational beacon, then we can safely keep The Group as supreme and function successfully in the planet-side trip. There are even non-safe groups that we can belong to such as Hell's Angels, the Communist party, the John Birch Society, and various other militant and rebel groups scattered throughout the country. We can select any group as The Group. The zoology of groups that function supreme is multifarious and polymorphous.

BOND RELEASE

Crowds of humans outside me push and pull me.

I get Close to 1, 2 or 3 and I'm bound.

My bond energy is high, I link by proximity.

Long ago I formed bonds with them, broke the bonds.

Bond energy, I know.

Release of bond energy by breaking a bond, I know.

Use of bond energy, in the bond, I think I know.

But do I?

Released bond energy, in the absence of bonds, I boast to myself I know.

Do I, really?

Uneasy when in the bond, bent on breaking, to obtain released energy, am I.

Once released, the energy is used all too short a time.

Misused energy.

Re-direction to what where I want to grow.

Where what is that?

Some of these groups are so well organized that they have lasted hundreds of years. Examples include various churches, the United States Government and various state, city, and small-town governments.

Business

Corporations and other organizations such partnerships and individuals doing business with one another, know well how to use the group as controller. A successful business is a successful group operating as a unit, usually under the leadership of one or two strong individuals. However, in a strong, large corporate structure, there need not be strong individual leaders; there can be an interlocked oligarchy that, in effect, runs the corporation.

Looked at from the outside, any large corporation is such an immense feedback system of many individuals working in concert that short of a complete systems analysis, no individual within the corporation can tell you where all the power actually resides. The power to make decisions, to set strategy, and so forth, may not be where it appears to be. An operations analysis of a large corporation and the corporations with which it does business can show tilt points and places where energy can be shifted by putting the proper information in the proper hands.

NO INDIVIDUAL WITHIN THE CORPORATION CAN TELL YOU WHERE ALL THE POWER ACTUALLY RESIDES.

Good Ol' Boys

Women are still expected to take a back seat, so that business women continue to be paid less than men to do the same job and have less power than men within almost any business organization. Most organizations of any kind in the United States are boys' clubs; there are a few girls' clubs, and a very few boy-and-girl clubs. Most of those that pretend to be boy-and-girl clubs seem to be run sub-rosa by the men involved.

This boys' club model carries on all the way up through the highest levels of the government. The number of women who have served in the United States Congress, in the cabinet, in executive positions throughout the bureaucracy of the United States Government is very small indeed. The same applies to the United Nations and to the administration of most of our schools. With very few exceptions men's groups run the politics, business, and education of our nation.

Big Brother

Much modern government is fast becoming a very patriarchal source of loving compassion. The government is progressively taking more and more responsibility of individuals for themselves away from them and granting it to groups of so-called "experts". For example, the Federal Food and Drug Administration (FDA) decided that certain biofeedback devices have to be sold on prescription. It looks as though even our brain waves are subject to government control. We are not allowed a peek at our own brain waves except under the auspices of a member of the medical profession.

Group pressure expressed through government, acting back upon the individual, can wield the stamp of "illegal" in order to "protect the public interest". In other words, this pressure group has assumed that the rest of the population are idiots who will not learn how to take care of themselves with modern drugs or modern inventions of various sorts; and yet it is quite willing to allow each of these "idiots" to drive vehicles at high speeds without such effective controls. Even safety devices on cars express the patriarchal aspect of government. The buzzers for seat belts and brakes and doors are a continuing expression of the father-like care that the government is taking of its citizens. In effect, the group is saying: "There is no such thing as individual responsibility; The Group will take responsibility for each of us."

Group Think states: if you do not agree with our *res* for our taking responsibility for you, we will fine you and put you in jail. If you attempt to take responsibility for yourself, we will make a criminal out of you. This is true not only for automobiles and drugs, but for possessing, selling and distributing certain weeds, plants, and medical devices.

Mind Police

One group activity that has been shown to be truly effective is the control by The Group of the states of consciousness of the individual. A given group will say: "There are certain states of consciousness which we expect of you; there are other states of consciousness which we expect you not to go into. These are forbidden states of consciousness".

Certain states of consciousness are to be forbidden because only saints, mystics, and far-out people from the Far East are permitted to go into them. There is to be no bliss, no ecstasy, no nirvana, no Samadhi, no satori, except under very

FROM THE MYTHIC TIME OF OUR FIRST ANCESTORS, WE HAVE LIVED UNDER A NEAR CONSTANT ASSAULT AIMED AT CURIOSITY, AT KNOWING, AT DARING TO EXPLORE ONESELF AND ONE'S WORLD, AT CLAIMING ONE'S BODY AND MIND AS ONE'S OWN.

—RICHARD GLEN BOIRE
On Cognitive Liberty

carefully controlled conditions permitted under the authority of The Group.

In another area there are groups which insist on group sexual activities, for example. These exert influences just as powerful upon individuals in The Group as do more conventional groups. Group loyalty is to be expressed by being discreet with outsiders about group activities. Persons to be selected as new members are to be selected by all group members; any one person can blackball any potential new member. Any current member can be thrown out of The Group by a sufficient vote against that member. Of course in reality any person the leadership does not like can be ousted and the leadership can act "as if" the decision were a group decision.

The Law

The law is one concomitant of group activity that we all face. The legal system, the police, the courts, the penal system all have been carried over from the past and are presented to us, as we grow up, as *fait accomplis*. The enactment of new laws applicable to all citizens equally can at best provide some of us with useful guidelines for individual and group behavior. What should concern us is the climate in which such laws can be sponsored and enacted. Frequently legislatures, frightened by a climate of panic, have voted into law measures they should have examined more objectively. The New American Patriot Act with all of its complexity, for example, was ratified with only one dissenting vote less than a week after the 9/11 terrorists attacks on the World Trade Center.

Laws passed under conditions of panic can be like the laws the young pass in their own mind under such conditions. They are extreme reactions to what is thought to be an emergency that will last eternally; they replace careful examination of the root causes and the effect of a given set of happenings. Laws passed in a state of national hysteria can lead to negative national programs and the creation of opposition in nation undergrounds.

Nations

Practically no one individual can possibly understand what it is that motivates a group mind of the size of a nation by the time the group gets to be that size. When hundreds of millions of people together have the kind of organization called a "nation," effective understanding of the interrelated facets of that organization becomes an awesome burden. We can see how episodes like World War II and the Vietnam and Korean wars got started. When, for reasons of national security, there is a definite policy for preventing the transmittal of certain kinds of information to the body politic, then we can see that individuals caught up in the group think of government itself, especially those isolated at the top by their own group think processes, can lead us down paths we may later regret having traveled.

The immense complexity of feedback patterns in terms of money flow and power within such groups is incredibly hard to understand. When we extend the concept of the nation to the whole planet and see the multiplicity of human types within nations, the polymorphous, continuous, multiple feedbacks based on differing belief systems throughout the planet become tremendously difficult set of processes to understand.

Navigating Group Pressure

What is the individual to do in the face of group pressure? First of all, we can examine within ourselves the instructions dictating behavior within given groups that we have acquired. We can very carefully scan such instructions from our infantile, childhood and adolescent years. We can examine the laws legislated for us that are not consonant with a full and satisfying life on our planet. We can examine our current group relationships and see how much we are paying for the benefits we receive from the group.

A realistic attribution of the privileges, property, or relationships derived through our own effort versus that of our group memberships must be established. It is a necessity that we be strong enough and free enough to pause and take a good look at what we owe to whom in terms of individual and group activity.

Examine in Solitude

Through isolation of ourselves from all groups for an hour or more each day for weeks, months, even years, we will acquire what can be acquired no other way, a grounding platform for functioning within groups.

Examining the power of The Group within us is a cleansing and creative process. If you have the advantages of an isolation tank, or of a room in which you can be alone under sensory reduced and isolated conditions, you can look at the internal structure of your mind, your beliefs and their relationship to groups of various sorts. You can look at your family relationships, your business, church, or club relationships, your government or military organization relationships, your medical or dental relationships—all the various aspects of your planet-side trip in which you are considered a member of various groups. There are times while in solitude, isolation and confinement when it looks as if we are nothing but a cross-correlated member of multiple groups with no other reality.

As we devise more and better means of getting off the planet and looking at it from outer space, we begin to obtain a more accurate perspective, to acquire a new set of priorities. We see that certain kinds of activities on the planet are not essential for improving the lot of human kind. We see that the use of poisons, weapons, and violence is a means of regulating the total population and doing this in a non-evolving fashion.

As we leave Planet Earth and look back at our human activities we realize that from a mere hundred miles out our presence on our planet is very hard to detect. We can see that in terms of our solar system our activities are not very important. Our most horrendous explosions are hardly noticeable on the next planet. The largest of our hydrogen bombs makes a flash that, if somebody happens to be looking in the right direction at the right time, might be seen across our solar system but would not be seen at all farther out in our galaxy.

We do not know how large a galactic group we are members of. The galaxy itself may have groups that are watching and caring about what our groups are doing. Or it may not. If we are going to project ourselves, where we are connected to other entities in this galaxy we do so through science.

PURSUING SEX

We are highly evolved **apes** with a medium-sized cerebral cortex, with built-in urges to survive and to propagate the species. When sexual stimulants, feelings, and activities are of supreme importance we are not able to take an objective look at what we are and cannot objectively examine our beliefs concerning sex and how it directs our lives.

When caught up by the current media treatment of sex as pornography or obscenity or as something to be transmitted via movies, tabloids, or slick magazines or is turned on to the special clothing, instruments and drugs that can excite and heighten sexual pleasure, or by the availability of sexual companions at a price, then you have a metabelief that having sex is the ultimate activity to seek after. Christian, the self-absorbed plastic surgeon of the popular *Nip and Tuck* TV series epitomizes the person who navigates his life by a belief in sex as the supreme pursuit. Marilyn Monroe is a well-known female example.

When captivated by this belief system, sexuality **is** separated from the rest of life. It is a special system created by The Group who wants to sell it and nurtured by The Group who buys it.

Hard-Wired

Each one of us has a basic biocomputer with built-in survival programs and built-in sexual programs. The purpose for these sexual programs is reproduction of the species, which, without birth control, is the likely result of so-called "normal" heterosexual activities of the healthy young. As we age, with more and more trips around the sun, we realize that these urges do not necessarily have the importance they assumed when we were younger.

As we age we see mysteries where before there were only certainties; we view the wellsprings of pleasure and pain more as subjects of speculation than powerful urges compelling us into certain kinds of activity. The young, however, in responding to their urges to mate, to make love, to reach orgasm, to reproduce, are merely performing these activities to meet the demands of their hard-wired sexual programs.

With the male the processes of sexual arousal, tumescence, orgasm with ejaculation, and detumescence are the stages in a special program that, once started, goes all the way to completion from sexual arousal to final orgasm with ejaculation. Many years ago, in working with electrodes in the brains of monkeys, I demonstrated that these processes are not necessarily hooked into the same parts of the central nervous system. I showed that there are separate sets of subroutines for each of these phenomena. Stimulating one area would cause erection but not orgasm or ejaculation. Stimulating another area would cause ejaculation but not erection or orgasm. Stimulating a third area would cause orgasm but not erection or ejaculation. I also found a central nervous system in which all three processes followed one after the other in the expected slavish fashion.

Humans, especially males, have experimented with separating these sexual processes one from the other. Success in this becomes easier as we ages. The urgency of youth galloping to orgasm-ejaculation is no longer present; there are alternatives.

In the human female the sexual processes are much less obvious and much less definite and generally are inclined to be somewhat entangled with her nest-building proclivities. However, there are exceptions. In *The Happy Hooker* Xaviera Hollander insists that women, once liberated from the old programs, can really enjoy sexual activities without any necessity of their being hooked up to propagation, children, and nest building. In addition, she says that the female has more staying power than the male to achieve multiple orgasms without fatigue, whether initiated from the clitoris or from the vagina.

Sexual Energy

Like money, so-called "sexual energy" can be used for many different purposes. It does not have to follow the arousal-to-orgasm script programmed into our biocomputer. Both man and woman can use "sexual energy" for purposes other than the direct expression of sexuality.

The rituals of Tantric Yoga, for example, introduced us to methods of holding off orgasm and maintaining sexual arousal over very long

WE CAN USE SEXUAL ENERGY FOR PURPOSES OTHER THAN THE DIRECT EXPRESSION OF SEXUALITY.

periods of time. When we achieve these goals, we see how flexible sexual energy really can be. We can shift it, as it were, from the basic biological substrate and the very narrow railroad-track program of the usual sexual encounter, to something far more complex — almost abstract and quite mystical.

If you follow the Tantric Yoga rituals very carefully you will find you can attain the so-called higher states of consciousness through sexual arousal and the forestalling of orgasm and ejaculation. Of course, in all such pursuits those attuned to the program of Pursuit of Orgasm and Sex as Supreme must be well aware that their biocomputers are so constructed as to over-value pleasurable states resulting from sexual activity. Almost as a hard-wired guarantee of propagation of the species, this program seems to reoccur again and again in different texts.

Thus, when we pursue the Tantric Yoga path, for example, we attain regions of very high feeling and very high-energy states in which we feel almost like we are achieving union with our Creator. Such high-energy states are useful in terms of exploring far-off spaces.

Robert Anton Wilson in *Sex and Drugs* underscored the fact that certain chemical substances, such as *Cannabis sativa* and LSD-25, mobilize and allow a more prolonged enjoyment of sexual activities and sexual activation. These substances turn on our emotional amplifiers and turn up their intensity control so that it is easy to achieve high-energy states of a sexual nature while under the influence of such entheogens. Some people are quite capable of moving themselves into sexual spaces, up to the edge of orgasm, and holding that space for a period of up to four, even six hours.

If you have done this, you may say, "So what?" The ability to delay orgasm is made possible because the biocomputer controls a great reservoir of sexual energy, which it releases under the influence of certain chemical substances. For those who worship Orgasm and Sex as the ultimate Truth, this kind of information is useful for a while. Later it all seems rather obvious and you will probably drop the whole program, again as aging takes place.

The classical Polynesian culture, for example, the belief system is that sexual activity is part of growing up; it is part of social life, and it should not be taken as seriously as it is in our culture. To the Polynesian, sex is fun, part of life, a series of fun games rather than a serious business. In cultures where this view obtains, there is no such thing as pornography.

In my own experience I have found that highly aroused sexual feelings prevented from going full cycle sometimes lead me into far-out spaces outside my body. Certain mystical states of consciousness share a good deal of this quality of sexual arousal "beyond sex," if you wish to put it that way. Whether this is another kind of energy that is aroused through the sexual, or whether it is sexual energy itself, is a moot point. The high energy states of consciousness of an extra-ordinary variety seem to be vastly pleasurable high energy states which somehow or other are beyond sex.

This feeling that they are beyond sex may, of course, come from our Western preprogramming by mystics or philosophers such as St. Theresa of Avila, St. John of the Cross, and Martin Buber. Freud felt that all the described states they mention were sublimated sexual states. Jung, on the other hand, was not so sure. He felt that there were far more states than mere sexual arousal.

Transposition of States

Central nervous system energy can be expressed in many different ways, with sexual energy being among the more compelling. We can initiate the arousal of sexual energy by the usual method — stimulation of breasts, penis, vagina or clitoris — and then move into other states of consciousness through this arousal if we can transpose it from the sexual system to other systems, avoiding in the process the obvious programs of sex itself. Once we achieve this kind of transposition, then the energy can be moved not only throughout the body but also into other people outside ourselves. But until we can apply it to our work, for example, or to some other productive activity, we will be caught up by narrow programming of our sexual energy.

After we achieve this moving about of energy, the energy apparently becomes unrecognizable as the "original force". Cerebral cortical control over the energy systems of the brain itself becomes so expert that it is almost as though there is no more need for pushing sexual systems as such. The pleasurable extremes of energy and sensation are not only those of orgasm.

As we become exposed to metaprograms which say, "No matter what happens, remain conscious and record the experience", as we are better and better at this art of maintaining consciousness in the presence of extreme levels of pleasure or extreme levels of pain, we are more able to enter new regions of experience and of mystery.

WHEN WE BREAK LOOSE FROM THE AUTOMATIC PROGRAMMING OF THE BIOCOMPUTER, THAT ENERGY IS AVAILABLE FOR OTHER PURPOSES.

As soon as we break loose from the automatic programming of the biocomputer in the body, the energy of that biocomputer is available to us for new purposes. Thus, we can see that pursuing orgasm as a navigational beacon is a very limiting belief. This is believing that the railroad-track simplicity of the human body is the be-all and end-all of the universe.

This may be true or not true. If you believe it to be true, however, it definitely is true for you. But let us put aside sexual energies for the moment and talk about the belief in Love as a supreme guide.

LOVE SUPREME

Love of the infant variety, which includes love for the mother and the father, love of parents by the child, love of other children by the child, love of the adolescent. These are slowly maturing sets of programs. In the first case, the infant's love is based upon pleasure and survival in that pleasure. If early infants receive too much pain they die. Love is essential for an infant's survival. For adolescents, love is more of a self-assertion. If adolescents do not know anything else, then out of this ignorance they may follow the dictates of the reproductive urges and produce children.

During the processes of maturation, however, some energy may be diverted, to be used extra-curricularly, if you wish, in becoming enamored of knowledge or technique, of thinking or of doing.

There is a belief system of love as a supreme guide which forbids orgasm. This is the typical celibate program of the Catholic Church, of various schools of Yoga, of the so-called brabmacharya trip, and so on. These schools attempt to bypass the demands of the biocomputer, putting them down as belonging to our "lower animal nature". In this belief, if you indulge in sexual intercourse — make love — then you necessarily cannot achieve a high spiritual state, whereas if you forego sexual intercourse a high spiritual state will automatically result from the deprivation.

This belief system works to a certain extent for some persons and not at all for others. A friend explained to me that in the state of brahmacharya — abstinence from sexual intercourse — most of his thinking was about sex. In effect, he was flooded by sex by forbidding it to himself. However, as he got older and the force of his biocomputer urges decreased, the brabmacbarya trip was much easier to achieve. Interestingly, those who are on this trip show an intense, youthful enthusiasm for whatever it is they are doing, which is considered to be a substitute for the sexual trip. There is an infectious freshness about them, especially about those who are carrying it out successfully.

MUCH OF LEARNING IS DOING THAT WHICH WE WILL NEVER DO AGAIN.

Some persons who have had a very active sex life and then in their later years are forced into the brahmacharya state because of the death of their mate, either find a new mate or tend to die off slowly. Their belief is that sexual experience is synonymous with being alive.

Brahmacharya does not seem to be the answer for most people. If these people could be induced to change their basic belief systems, it is possible that they would take on whole new programs related to the use of their basic energies. The use of these energies is one of the stickiest areas of human striving, filled with ambivalence, judgmental attitudes, and destructive judgments, actions, and feelings.

It is important to realize that the effect of sexual activity in our biocomputer operations is transitory. Although after sexual intercourse we feel an easing of tension, a renewed concentration of thought in desired areas, a certain relief from the biological urges within us, the sexual urges eventually rise again in their incessant march toward fulfillment. By keeping this aspect of our biocomputer satisfied, we can avoid worshiping orgasms. For most persons this seems to be the most satisfactory course.

The Dyad

If I fall passionately in love with somebody at least for a while that person holds the supraself-metaprogrammatic position and is therefore necessary for the "highs" of my higher states of consciousness. My thought processes are preoccupied with my relationships with that individual, with her beauty, with her divinity of form, with the perfections of her thinking, feeling, doing. For me her smile is a long period of good weather, the way she walks is the most perfect way the universe has ever devised, her self-metaprogrammer is the most nearly ideal one I have ever met, and her supraself-metaprograms are a perfect match for my own.

> **THE PERSON ONE LOVES NEVER REALLY EXISTS, BUT IS A PROJECTION FOCUSED THROUGH THE LENS OF THE MIND ONTO WHATEVER SCREEN IT FITS WITH LEAST DISTORTION.**
>
> **—ARTHUR C. CLARKE**
> *Tales of Ten Worlds*

In such a passionate dyad many things occur which we could hope would occur among all human beings consistently and over longer periods of time. In general this over-evaluation of a given individual making that individual into a god or a goddess seems to be a part of growing up. We talk about infantile love, childish love, adolescent love, and finally, mature love. The infant, child and adolescent love make the mistake of making a God out of another human. They also are a learning platform from which we make progress in the proper assignment of supraself-metaprograms in the proper areas. We have to make the mistake, as it were, of assigning this to at least one human being, unconsciously, before we realize consciously that we have done so. Much of learning is doing that which we will never do again.

BEYOND "REPRODUCE!:

SUPRASELF DYAD

We, in this dyad, each have already reproduced.

You have children made, a have I, each with another, not us.

You can no longer become pregnant.

With you I cannot impregnate.

We can love, fuck, ecstatic union.

After many such, what then?

Are we here for sensation's sake?

Can we go beyond, through us and sex?

Where is "beyond"?

Far out spaces, greater beings—entities than us, beckon and call.

Together can we go to them, or is it each of us alone?

Let us try, together, to so go.

Let us face our hindrances, evasions, blocks, and soar, together.

The hindrance of body ecstasy tied here convert to spirit travel energy there.

The hindrance of planet earth, mother ties to her bosom, use constructively.

The evasion of loss of independent self, convert to dyad greatness.

Together fusing into one to travel as two-in-one.

No rivalry, no control for each separate over other, one directed by each of two, fused.

A dream, a fantasy? Poetry?

No.

A program, a metaprogram for a Supra-self dyad.

I sever, I distinguish, I cross, I call, I name.

The universe of confusion is mapped, navigated, I pilot myself through it.

A pilot, a navigator, an engine appear, for the engine an engineer

The I-Me spaces distinguish and sever themselves into

"I pilot, I navigate, I furnish the energy, the engine.

I move, I cross, I map, I name, I call.

So Inner Universes I can explore.

Now I can communicate with you."

Making our beloved into a god is a lesson to be learned, a stage in our progress toward mature understanding of the relationship between the self-metaprogrammer and the supraself-metaprograms. We worship and venerate something else.

When I try to think in terms of my relationship with Toni, my wife — the dyad — my thinking becomes non-egocentric and dyado-centric. Dyado-centric thinking is hard to conceptualize alone. It can quite easily be done by the dyad because the dyad is then functioning. The group mind of two is far greater than the mind of one. One alone can go on talking and talking and yet never arrive at the talking of two. "Without you, there is no us. I am I, you are you, we are we, without you I am only I, with you I become an US". It is the attempt to use this kind of thinking without being consciously aware of it that generates such institutions as marriage and families. Most love affairs start with the young trying to understand that the dyad is greater than either of the individuals but the individuals thrashing around within the dyad are still more egocentric than they are dyado-centric.

ONE ALONE CAN GO ON TALKING AND TALKING AND YET NEVER ARRIVE AT THE TALKING OF TWO.

When Toni and I met I realized that here was a woman with whom I could give up my egocentric motivations and become a dyado-centric individual. More accurately, I had attempted this at least twice before in my life in two previous marriages and had not succeeded. I had succeeded temporarily, but the relationships required too much energy and too much constant awareness, detracting from the other projects in which I was immersed. However, I must credit my two previous wives, Mary and Elizabeth, with being excellent teachers in the dyadic sense. Even as we all do, they brought with them into the dyad their ego-centricity, their ego motivation.

Toni was an extremely well-grounded, well-centered, magnificent, broad-minded, tolerant, diplomatic woman. She turned out not to be as tolerant as she thought she was, however. She disliked certain people and did not want to be near them even if I had a liking for the same people, but that is rather rare. There were a few individuals, usually women from my previous life, whom Toni would put up with. I must say that she did not thrust the men of her previous life on me unless there is a mutual interest and a mutual willingness to have them in our environment.

CONTRACT: ME AND THEE

Do you want to live with me, I with you?

If we do so want, let us see.

If we live dyadically, then we interlock.

We share joy in sexual ways.

We talk of likes and dislikes.

I, without knowing, take on some of yours.

You, mine.

I look at him, her, and hear echoes of your opinion, as if my own. You look at him, her, and hear mine as if yours.

We share our human maps of humans.

Each takes on, one the other's maps.

Do I like/wish to have your maps without awareness?

Do you like/wish to have mine?

In you, maps for yourself, do you have transcendence of
your today's self and your today's maps?

If not, forget me, us.

If so, let us see together if you wish and work to transcend you, and if I wish and work to transcend me.

Can we together transcend the us, of now?

Where, when, how?

The farther out I went, the more Toni held on to her
gardening, to her rug hooking, to her Karma Yoga.
However, without her presence I could not go out
quite so far, and I must say she was a great attraction
for coming back to this planet, to this life, to this body.
In one episode in which I almost drowned, I was in a
hot pool at the time, stood up too fast, and fell facedown. At that moment there was a telephone call for
me and Toni came out to get me. She saw me floating
in the pool, still facedown, and immediately began
mouth-to-mouth resuscitation. She then went to find
Will Curtis, who called the sheriff. Very soon after, a
helicopter came and took me to the hospital.

This story illustrates two things. The first: we cannot always be aware that a very simple thing can kill
us. In a case such as mine, standing up too fast can
bring on what is called "hypostatic anemia". This is
the effect of diffusing blood into the capillaries which
are in the periphery and are already dilated with the
heat which is threatening the brain's intactness. When
I stood up, the blood shifted from the brain out into
these other blood vessels temporarily and before the
beat could pump it back, the brain stopped operating
and I lost consciousness.

The second thing that the incident illustrates is that my faith in Toni was well borne out. At critical times she heard my unconscious call for help and responded to it. This may look like a "coincidence." Coincidence is one interpretation of what happened, but for when I look at the events themselves, there is no such thing. Coincidence is the name that, in order to explain them, we fasten to events that somehow occur in a proper sequence to bring about a result.

My first impression of Toni as an eagle-like character has also been fully borne out. She possessed a vast reservoir of serene contemplation, of peace, of physical vigor and of an ability to demand and hold onto the ties to the land that her Sicilian Albanian ancestors have always demanded. She was delightful in her physical appearance, in the brightness of her smile she so constantly expressed. She had a deep interest in others and in her beloved Los Angeles. She had the warm heart of the Mediterranean peoples, and yet she fully appreciated my less emotional northern Minnesota English/Welsh/German background. We complemented each other in many ways, and every day was a set of new discoveries of the delights of our dyad.

HERE AND NOW
WITHOUT THEE

Where are you now? Not with me, away. There's an ache, a longing, an empty place. When you are near you fill something. That something is blankness now. I grieve, I cry, I try to fill the something.

I seek others they can't fill.

I seek another, smother her, poll away.

She's not you, who have filled that place.

To seek, to find another: can I?

I can, but something won't yet let go of you.

The limbo of me, of you, far away.

Why a limbo?

You left, planning your trip, extending it.

What secret thing in you needed the trip?

I did not ask the secret. I do not ask now.

I cannot invade your private reasons.

They are yours, not mine, not ours.

I watched you grow, planning your trip.

Your growth I felt and cherished.

We played the game of letting each other.

Letting go, adult acceptance of adult decision.

The cost I feel, the cost I pay, for letting.

Brief regrets—but there was no alternate path,

I thought.

You travel around the planet's surface, all the way.

I am anchored here, committed to remain here.

We are split into two, one traveling.

DEATH AS THE END

Insofar as is known through our present-day science, no one of us is immortal. Each one of us must face our own death. Most of us would find it difficult to follow consciously Don Juan's advice to Carlos Castaneda: "Keep death at your left hand". Rather, most of us generally attempt to avoid a realization that our own end must come, leaving such considerations for times when we are depressed or 'being philosophical".

How we face our death at the time that it has become imminent will depend upon our belief systems operating at that particular time. If we believe that death is the end of us as an individual — the total, utter and complete end — then we will face our death with a set of feelings and realizations different from any set we previously had.

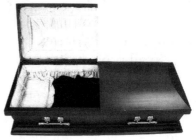

Let us take a good look at the belief in death as "the end".

According to this set of beliefs, we are born into the world as a result of the sexual activities of our parents; we live out our life span as a biological organism and eventually die either through accident, disease, the operations of other people, or what we call "old age".

HOW WE FACE OUR DEATH WILL DEPEND UPON OUR BELIEF SYSTEMS OPERATING AT THAT PARTICULAR TIME. Most persons have been exposed to a view of death taken from some organized religion, a view that tells us that our body will die but our soul will go somewhere else for judgment, eventually to rejoin the body, which on the day of final judgment will rise again from the ground in which it is buried.

This belief system dominates Christian industries that thrive on death. We are expected to buy or lease a plot of ground into which our body is to be placed at the end of life. Our survivors are expected to have that body embalmed and otherwise prepared by morticians to be as lifelike looking as possible for the wake. At the funeral, all our relatives and friends are expected to gather to mourn our departure. Thus do the industries which market coffins, floral arrangements, cemetery plots, and so forth, thrive on the Death belief system Jessica Mitford described in her best seller, *The American Way of Death.*

Many Hazards

What the cause of our own death will be is in all probability quite indeterminate. We are surrounded in modern civilization by countless potentially lethal devices and lethal situations, day in and day out. In California, for example, it is quite impossible to say when, and if, a very large earthquake may occur, wiping us out along with tens of thousands of other people. Anytime we drive a car at high speed on a freeway, we are placing ourselves in jeopardy. In the ordinary home there are plenty of opportunities to be electrocuted, burned, suffocated, or poisoned. So, we do live with death at our left hand, even though we usually ignore it.

The Soul

Those who have been through a close brush with death followed by a long period of recovery in which they had a hard look at the possibilities of dying, are in a better-than-average position to question their belief system regarding Death. There have been cases where a person is suddenly thrown into a coma for causes which he doesn't know, even though others outside his body can easily see it is due to an encephalitis virus which shoots up body temperature, a cerebral vascular accident, a bad fall with a blow to the head, a head-on automobile smashup, or leaking gas while he was asleep, as examples.

The outside view of what happens to us under such grave circumstances is not at all like the inside view of what happens under these circumstances. I have collected many firsthand accounts of close brushes with death and have asked specifically about the inside experiences. I recounted my own close scrapes with death in *The Center of the Cyclone*.

To summarize, most people experience a set of realities entirely different from external realities during a period of traumatic unconsciousness. Of course we have been able to get accounts only from survivors of a near death experience (NDE). In general, the inside view is that there are realities in which we do not have a body, or the necessity for a body, but do have our intelligence,

NDE's GIVE A GLIMPSE OF A REALITY THAT SEEMS TO BE ENDLESS, ETERNAL, AND REPEATING. memories, consciousness and emotions. So we are a complete individual, extra-body, "sans body".

This individual — the Self — exists in realities in which there are other entities like the Self. NDE's give a glimpse of a reality that seems to be endless, eternal, and repeating. There are rumors that there is no death in these regions, that we go on eternally and can do other things besides inhabiting a human biovehicle. To the people with these sets of experiences, the human body is merely a temporary abode for something else which classically, in Christian theology, is called the "soul". I call it the "essence". In Yoga terms it is the "atman," and so forth. These kind of experiences are cross-cultural and have been recorded in various parts of the world and interpreted in various ways according to the belief systems current at the time.

In some instances the feeling is that we have left a temporary proprietorship of a human condition and returned to a much more generalized abstract condition in which we are part of a vast general purpose.

The alternatives in this second state of existence are much greater than those that exist when in the human body. Access to knowledge is freer, unimpeded by human considerations. We are more objective, more understanding, more loving than when in the human body. We can also suffer more in this state if we must.

We can go through Heavens, we can go through Hells, and we can go through states of High Indifference. If we approach this state centered within our own knowledge and belief systems, then we can move through the state and back out again much more intact than if we had had no preprogramming in regard to approaching this state. Those who have been in this state for a sufficient period of time and have studied the results in sufficient depth come to the belief that death is not supreme, and we do not "die" in the usual sense.

Rather death is an opening, a way out, a transcendence of the human condition. As I have often said, recounting my own experiences under a condition of abstraction, "I do not feel that in this state I am facing God; I feel more that I am facing people in His 'outer office,' that there are many steps between me and God still left to accomplish".

With experiences such as these we hardly need to buy a cemetery plot or a coffin. We need only, as it were, to think of getting lost at sea, of being totally destroyed in some catastrophe that leaves no body to worry about, or to opt for cremation. In reality, of course, after such experiences, what happens to the body is totally unimportant and tends to be left to relatives and friends, hoping they will not face a financial burden and that their own belief systems will enable them to carry on in spite of our "apparent death".

RATHER DEATH IS AN OPENING, A WAY OUT, A TRANSCENDENCE OF THE HUMAN CONDITION.

When we tune in on the high-energy communications networks in special states of consciousness, we are reassured by the then-existing fact that we are a node in such a network; that there is constant information being fed into us, being computed below our levels of awareness and transmitted to others. This is all done with extremely high energy, far above what we usually experience while in ordinary states of consciousness in the body. We experience streamings of energy from unknown sources; streamings of energy going toward unknown sinks. A few of the nearby other nodes in the network may be visible.

We Are More

In such states there is no body, there is only pure streaming energy, carrying information. In such a state we suddenly realize that we are far more than we assumed we were when in the body, and yet we are also far less in terms of ego. In this state we are a "cosmic computer" connected into the rest of the cosmic computers and into a huge universal computer. During such experiences we feel the connections between all these computers as love, respect, awe, reverence, curiosity and interest. And, yet, there is a high degree of efficiency with which the traffic is handled in these information channels.

In such a state we realize that we have existed for several millions of years, that again and again and again we have taken on some form in addition to this cosmic computer form—in short, that we have transmigrated again and again and again, not necessarily only as a human being. There is a huge backlog of experience available to us if we can only tap into the storage mechanisms for these memories. At certain points it is as if the memories were not our own but were a central, universal store in which such information is carried through the centuries and the millennia.

After such experiences I can no longer feel that I cease to be when my body dies. The "reality" of the end of the self is no longer looming. Somehow I am committed to a much broader view than the egoistic, solipsistic, body-centered belief system common in the human being.

WE ARE FAR MORE THAN WE ASSUMED WE WERE WHEN IN THE BODY, AND YET WE ARE ALSO FAR LESS IN TERMS OF EGO.

Whether this is merely another set of beliefs that generate certain experiences when out of contact with the body, I don't know. I have no secure way of separating traveling among my own simulations within my own programmatic spaces from a true set of experiences having to do with universal communication. Each of us may end with the death of our brain. On the other hand, my belief in this belief is not as secure as it used to be; it has been disturbed by my experiences. My disbelief in my continuance beyond the death of my body has been weakened. My belief that we have, by happenstance, totally originated as biological organisms on this planet is no longer as strong as it used to be.

I could easily say that with knowing about the new belief systems of exploration and of finding the realities that lie adjacent to, superimposed upon, and inherent in the reality I faced with every day, I could have more than one alternative. There is a saying in yachting that the skipper should never be caught with just one alternative. So, when we face our death, we should have a number of alternative belief systems at our disposal. This is only practical, wouldn't you agree?

If you have only one belief system regarding death and if that is that you end with the death of your body, then you might well become rather desperate at the time of your death, although even then death can be faced and accepted with dignity, with love, and with compassion. As soon as death becomes something that we can grasp, can think about, explore, and deal with, rather than a wrathful and judgmental nothingness to be faced at the end of our present physical being, then we can become much more optimistic about our sojourn on this planet.

BODY

Each year billions of dollars are spent on entertainment, athletics, care of the body, cosmetics and other beauty aids, physical fitness, golf, football, baseball, worship of superstars, of music, TV and movies, on yoga, Tai Chi Chuan, Kung Fu, karate, jujitsu, judo, aikido, swimming pools, tennis courts, mountain climbing, camping, skiing, water skiing, sailing, surfing, and so forth. In each of these activities a very high premium is placed on various aspects of bodily function and the appearance of our body to others. Very large numbers of people who indulge in these activities believe in the Body as steersman.

Thousands of Americans spend their weekend being physically active, and more and more thousands are becoming adherents of the physical-fitness cult, if only in terms of jogging or light morning exercises. The manufacture of sports equipment has become a large industry. The various techniques of body improvement, from Jack LaLanne to Yoga classes and the various so-called martial arts, are big business.

Let us try to get at the basic factors involved in the belief system that the Body is supreme. First of all, whether we like it or not in our more idealized moments, we are a walking, running, climbing animal. Unless we perform these activities, our body deteriorates. Unless we work out equivalents for body toning in terms of stretching and stressing the body, the quality of our thinking, feeling and doing slowly but surely likewise deteriorates.

Many people exercise because they feel better as a consequence of the exercise. They can think, work, and play better. In the Far East this has been known for literally thousands of years. Stretching and stressing the body have become esoteric sciences. The best known of these, Hatha-Yoga, is touted as a doorway to spiritual advancement. Various martial arts: aikido, Kung Fu, karate, and so forth, are spiritual trips in various countries in the East. The "feeling better" that results from these activities is taken as an advance in personal discipline and in perfection of the body itself.

In the West there is a saying "A sound mind in a sound body," in other words, a sound mind results from generating a sound body. The body responds to a cyclical need for exercise and stretching. There is a daily cycle of twelve to twenty-four hours, and a weekly cycle of approximately seven days. If these cycles are studied in ourselves, we can find, for example, that we should devote a period to stretching early in the morning and another period late in the afternoon or before going to bed. On the weekends we should stress the whole organism, exerting physical effort to the extent we hyperventilate as a consequence of the muscular activity, and our heart rate and the heart beat volume are stepped up during this period of exercise. Without these the circulatory system and the respiratory system degenerate, and all the familiar processes of aging and disease take place.

One of the amazing things that we notice in the older teachers of Yoga and the martial arts is their extreme youthful appearance, even when they are old. A fifty-year-old looks like a thirty-year-old and an eighty-year-old looks decades younger. The obvious effects of aging, including either emaciation or over-weight, just do not occur in these people who have managed to keep these physical disciplines going over their life span. To be continuously effective disciplines they must be followed from youth to old age.

For those who practice these disciplines, what I am saying is obvious. For those who do not, what I am saying may be taken with a good deal of skepticism. In *The Dyadic Cyclone*, my wife Toni and I explain the minimum possible programs for the body, the stretching and stressing exercises, complete with a time schedule. These programs can be elaborated or extended.

It is wise to stress that in bodily development if your body is not in good shape, you must start slowly and not stretch or stress beyond the minimum discomfort level at the beginning. You can overdo it. The important metaprogram, the important general principle above all others, is to exercise a little bit every day up to your comfort limit. As practically everybody has found who has followed a proper stretching and stressing regimen there is a point at which it becomes fun. You can always push beyond your limits and make it not fun once again, no matter how good a condition you are in. You cannot only get a second wind, but a third, fourth, and a fifth wind, as it were.

These seem to be the physiological bases for the activity centered around the body. In addition to the basics of running, climbing, and walking, the necessity of stressing and stretching, there are less necessitous kinds of activities that go with the belief system that the body is the supreme temple. We can transfer the pleasure obtained from our body and its stretching and stressing to others who are better than we are in a given type of exercise. We can make a hero or a heroine out of those who have spent a professional life doing the kind of exercise that we are interested in.

We can worship the body and the mind of our Hatha-Yoga guru, of our aikido teacher, of our Tai Chi teacher, of our athletics coach, of professionals and amateurs in any sport. This kind of transference to another from ourselves, from our own body to another's, to our activities, is a learning procedure in childhood, adolescence and young adulthood. This identification with idealized persons who are doing better than ourselves seems to be a necessary step for most of us to achieve on our own. However, sometimes this worship of body, the belief in Body as supreme, becomes separated from our own accomplishments and we worship on a vicarious basis without doing anything about our own body. This vicarious worship accounts for the popularity of spectator sports rather than engaging in them ourselves.

Of course we can aspire to be a teacher of a given stretch or stressing set of exercises. We may then want to have vicariously the admiration that we see professionals getting; or we may simply feel that a kind of activity is so worthwhile that we want others to learn it. The thin line between the body as supreme and the planet-side survival trip as a professional teacher is a narrow boundary indeed. It is possible to flip over into complete worship as opposed to a balanced life. This is very easy to do with the body as the supreme belief system.

BEAUTY AS STEERSMAN

The beauty industry is an outgrowth of worshiping the body. This industry does not necessarily ground itself on a physical fitness basis, even though in our culture those in good physical shape—not too fat, not too thin, with adequate muscular development—are generally seen as the most beautiful bodies.

No one seems to know where our criteria of physical beauty arose. It is well known that the criteria of beauty in various parts of Africa are different from one another and from the European criteria. The differences of the human face and figure throughout the world extend across a fairly wide spectrum of form, color, texture, body weight per unit height, and so forth. The saying "Beauty is in the eye of the beholder" shows that most criteria of beauty are arbitrary programs inserted into our training while very young. To the very young everything is beautiful. It is only with the

MOST CRITERIA OF BEAUTY ARE ARBITRARY PROGRAMS INSERTED INTO OUR TRAINING WHILE VERY YOUNG. shaping by parents and peers and fantastic media presentations that we develop a narrow set of criteria for what we consider beauty.

Some people look beautiful when we first see them, whereas others become beautiful with continued contact and the appreciation gained by delving into their thinking, feeling, and doing. With some, we may realize with time that their beauty is of form rather than of substance and function, while with others the form is not formally beautiful but the mind and the spirit are beautiful. There are times when we can recapture the ecstatic, blissful state of the infant in which everything and everyone is beautiful. We can change our "eye of the beholder".

Those considered formally "beautiful" are hired by the advertising industry, by corporations, by government, by the movie and TV industries, to play the roles of public purveyors of beauty products, clothes, automobiles, and so forth. It is to be noticed, however, that these models of various races are selected not so much according to the criteria of the Africans, Asians, and so on, but according to Western criteria of formal beauty. Noses, eyes, lips, chin, jowls, are selected according to Western European/American criteria rather than racial/tribal criteria.

Formal beauty is so well stipulated that practically the whole beauty industry operates on the basis of one set of standards. When we look at *Vogue*, *Cosmo*, and other women's magazines, we see a uniformity of standards for women as well as for men. There are definite kinds of eye shadow, eyeliner, lipstick color, face powder, antiperspirant, toothpaste, shampoo, hair conditioner, body oil, feminine hygiene preparation, deodorant soap, nail polish color, and so forth.

Setting up the criteria for what a female should put on various parts of her face is almost an esoteric art. Should or should not she wear false eyelashes? Should or should not she wear lipstick? How long should she wear her hair in what sort of fashion? Should she change her hair color at this time? Are her clothing and face color coordinated?

Fat is Good

The value of fat for survival is dictated by factors not generally present in our society. For the best physical condition the body density should be as high as possible in our society. This leaves very little allowance for body weight loss in the case of illness. The weight lost in bed when one is ill is first the fat of the body. When this is all used up the muscle mass starts going. Hence you are losing protein, literally "eating" your own protein after "eating" your own fat. Thus it is wise to have some fat reserve.

The beauty industry specifies that "fat is ugly". There are some cultures in which "fat is beautiful". Traditionally, in Polynesia royalty are overfed until they become very fat and are thusly considered very beautiful. It was important that they be seen by their subject and being very fat made them easy to see. Another root of fat-as-beautiful belief may have been influenced by the long sea voyages of the Polynesians in which survival could depend upon being fat. If you must go without water for many days at a time, then it is best to be fat,

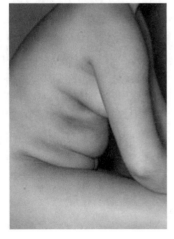

because you can burn the fat to carbon dioxide and
water, thus avoiding the necessity of taking in water.
The dolphins, whales, and porpoises do exactly this.
They are mammals living at sea without fresh water.
Another reason the Polynesians might have fattened
themselves for their voyages is the flotation that being
fat gained for them. If you are blown overboard, you
don't have to exert much effort to float if you are sufficiently fat.

For the Polynesians of today, however, there is no
such desperate need for being fat; consciously they
consider it an aesthetic thing rather than a survival
thing. It is imbedded in their culture because they
were brought up with the programming left over from
the time of the large migrations across the Pacific.

Another reason for staying fat is that there is more
to eat when one runs out of food under desperate conditions. Need for food intake does not arise as soon if
we are fat; we burn up—eat—our own fat. Secondly,
if a person dies or is killed while stranded with others or while adrift in a lifeboat, for example, there is
more for the others to eat if he is fat. This kind of thing
rarely happens nowadays, but it did happen: after a
crash landing in the mountains of Peru as described
in *Survive!* by Clay Blair, Jr. after the sinking of the
whale ship Essex, when the crew, having been forced
to the boats after a whale had destroyed the ship, ate
the body of the cabin boy as they drifted to the Chil-
ean coast during the expedition across the North Pole
by dirigible. Cannibalism in the service of survival is
not very well understood by those who have not been
faced with survival desperation. In his book, *The Boat*,
Walter Gibson presents a strong case in such circumstances

Survival Takes Precedence

Of course in all the above situations, the consideration of beauty disappeared, as is usually the case, under conditions of desperation, danger, and threats to survival. Under these circumstances, when we are under the sway of the survival programs within the biocomputer, beauty and its criteria are hardly important.

However, when we have taken the spiritual path and achieved a certain experience with various far-out states of consciousness, we begin to expand our criteria of beauty into regions where, before, they were almost forbidden. In these states of consciousness our criteria are so expanded that anything and everything becomes beautiful and perfect. We pull out of the human condition and the necessity for survival of the physical being and moves into eternal spaces united with all other sentient beings throughout the universe.

Beauty v. Ugliness

The impact of such experiences is so great that our criteria of beauty or of sin and virtue are completely flipped. We go through peculiar transformations in that what used to be considered beautiful expands to include many, many things that we might have considered ugly. Finally, the dichotomy "beauty and ugliness" disappears as we achieve a state of High Indifference in which we realize that bliss does not come from the outside world, it comes from within. We elicit our own bliss, we elicit bliss in others. We realize our own eternal nature and hence are no longer quite so subject to the survival programs of the biocomputer.

BLISS DOES NOT COME FROM THE OUTSIDE WORLD, IT COMES FROM WITHIN.

MONEY AS GUIDE

Money is important. Money buys the necessities for survival for individuals, for businesses, for corporations, for states, for nations. The whole of the modern Western world is based upon its ideas of money. International trade, the value of the dollar in Japan, in Western Europe and around the world, determines most people's lives and fortunes. Large amounts of money are so powerful that those who have them for any length of time surround themselves by safeguards, advisors, trusts and so on, to prevent the dissipation of that power. Those who have no money must get it in one form or another from private individuals, from state governments, or from the federal government.

The belief in the preeminence of money is a powerful determinant of behavior in our Western society. According to the usual social criteria, the misuse of money by private individuals and by public officials is on the list of sins. Those who blatantly steal money without surrounding their theft with all sorts of legal safeguards are subject to the severest penalties. Those who know how to obtain large amounts of money can make a very subtle priest-like game out of playing with their money. The aristocracy in the United States are those who have either inherited large amounts of wealth or have acquired large amounts of wealth in their lifetime.

Public officials in charge of grants, of disbursement of government funds and of the collection of government taxes, similarly are priests in the church of money. The taxation authorities have the power to examine the personal life of any individual citizen or of any corporation. Rules for the worship of money are quite stringent and specific, like any of the litanies, rituals and belief systems that have appeared in the Western world. Powers to jail those who do not adhere to the proper rituals, litany and paper work.

Money represents a flow of initiative from one person to another person. Money in capital savings represents frozen initiative, in the world of the paper realities. The fear of "getting down to one's last dollar" can be a source of high motivation for many people. Some people with this fear have made millions of dollars, and some of these have lost it all. Some of the latter have sacrificed their life for money, such as those who committed suicide during the 1929 crash of the stock market.

MONEY REPRESENTS A FLOW OF INITIATIVE FROM ONE PERSON TO ANOTHER PERSON.

Money Valve

Those who are in business must realize that they are "money valves". This condition is more obvious in business than it is in any other aspects of life. Perhaps you are starting a new business and have a certain amount of money to invest in this business. With a proper bookkeeper and a proper accounting firm, you can learn the "res" for investment, making a profit, paying taxes, meeting a payroll, and for all the other operations in the paper reality of any business. Those who have struggled to meet a payroll every month are a special club, which is not understood very well by those who are simply on payrolls that are met every month.

Business owners are money valves. They sell something, receive something from the public for it, and distribute that money to others, including employees, suppliers, sub-contractors, and so on. In the paper world of credit they have a quantitative rating, which determines fairly well how much money society will allow to flow through the businesses. If they are trustworthy, loyal, and have met their payroll for a number of years, their credit is good up to a certain limiting value. If they learn how to expand their value, or to open themselves up as a money valve, then their credit ratings **MONEY THEN IS NOT MERELY INITIATIVE; MONEY IS LITERALLY A MEASURE OF THE NUMBER OF ALTERNATIVES AVAILABLE TO US** can rise, which means that they are allowed a larger flow of money through their trustworthy organizations. One very peculiar thing about credit is that we must borrow money in order to establish credit. This is the usual case of the small business owners.

As the power of the money valve goes up and as we are entrusted with more and more money, then the *res* of the game changes. As we become one of those in control of the system—or the illusion of being in control—our ability to manipulate the lives of other people increases dramatically. This may be achieved through political means, corporate means with link-ups between corporations, through linkups with military plus the money market, or through the manipulation of large amounts of property. Certain new privileges appear that were not present at the lower levels of money flow. We now have the best possible advice from accounting, auditing and law firms. We have become a member of the privileged club.

Those who are born and raised in this belief system with sufficient amounts of money available can become a dissipated delinquent or they can turn the other way and become service-oriented, realizing that whatever money they have "they can't take it with them" and that it is a privilege given to them for this lifetime to be able to be of service to their fellow men. Those who are not subject to the necessity for making money can afford to give their services for worthy causes, whatever they may be—they may go into politics or into charity work; they may support the arts, a favorite school, a church. A person with money has many more alternatives than do people at the other end of the money spectrum. Money then is not merely initiative; money is literally a measure of the number of alternatives available to us, insofar as our external realities and social realities are concerned.

SELF-METAPROGRAM: MONEY

Money is what? Where does it come from, go?

Each is born—no money.

Each is raised—money? Pennies, nickels, dimes.

Older—quarters.

Suddenly—dollars.

Parents' money to each, to me.

My money—not hers, not his.

Candy, comics—I give money—I get my things.

I buy for my girl; she gives.

Buy, sell, give, for love of others.

Facilitator, friendship, credit: services,

Incoming $, outgoing

Bank account.

Books kept by bank, by me.

Credit: mine, theirs.

So I'm paid to do what they want me to do.

So I pay others to do what I want done.

I pay government—unless I do they take.

Things for money.

Money for things.

Service for money.

Money for service.

Love for money.

Money for love, love of money, money of love.

I am a money valve: it goes through me.

Money in, money out.

Too much in, or too much out: bad.

Just enough in, just enough out: good.

But keep money out less than money in.

A must.

But how judge future, money in-money out?

How much?

Hold some over, somehow, for future of avoiding too little-in, too much-out.

Money flows unless held.

Money held grows.

Money spent is gone.

Money held is future.

Past commitments use up present held money.

Here and now no outgoing money promises.

Here and now income promises, future income, through services, not things.

Here and now, no things for money, at least, minimize.

Here and now minimum bought services, maximum friendship performance.

Future credit to me,

Through love, and awareness of this program.

Minimize clothes, washing them.

New Breed of Wealthy

There is a new breed of wealthy men and women who are pursuing the inner paths. To pursue the inner life we must of necessity have a low public profile. Otherwise we become too involved in the affairs of the world and find great difficulty in establishing the necessary discipline to retire to the inside life.

There are also new life-styles in which we can devote several hours a day to the inside life and several hours a day to the outside life. If there are no money problems, the outside life can be one of service and teaching and the inside life one of seeking whatever it is that you seek.

If we are in the "bliss-programming" stage, then we bliss-program. If we are in the "exploratory inner universe" stage, then we explore the inner universes. If we are in the teaching mode, then we teach whomever and wherever we meet our students. If we want to become a powerful guru with a following, we can do that also. Those favored by having money thus have inner as well as outer alternatives not available to those not so favored.

The United States is the only country in the world in which a young rebel can make a phonograph record and earn several million dollars on the basis of a song that preaches rebellion against the Establishment. This is a refreshing new view of the relationship between young rebels and the society in which they live.

A well-known psychoanalyst, Robert Welder, said that "the United States is the first country in the world that has built-in a system of constant evolution without the need of violent revolution in order to change the structure of its establishment". The Constitution is a document that espouses evolution and balances power between various groups in such a way that there is a forced change built into the system. Thus anything I say, or that any other individual says, is subject to revision without notice.

The system in the United States is a living, growing organism, the parts of which do not understand the whole. To those most operative in this system,

MONEY IS A TOOL TO BE USED FOR THE GROWTH AND CHANGE OF THE INNER SOCIETY AS WELL AS THE OUTER SOCIETY. money is merely a means, not an end in itself. Money is a tool to be used for the growth and change of the inner society as well as the outer society. Services can be sold as well as goods; the mass production of services is a new industry running from advertising to spiritual trips, through a whole spectrum of software marketing. As we perfect a minimal standard of living and supply more and more people with this minimal standard of living, the software industries are going to be more and more important. As more of our material production becomes computer-controlled and computer-operated, so will the necessity for software for humans be expanded. More leisure time available will demand more services for the human participant.

Some spectacular things can be accomplished in the inner realities with the proper human software programming. Telling people how to do things inside their own heads has become a new industry in which fortunes are made — look at Wayne Dyer and Tony Robbins.

RIGHTEOUS WRATH
AS GUIDE

I have retained a habit from my youth of walking away when I am angry. This enables me to calm down and to work out whatever problem exists. But today I lost my temper. I justified it by saying that it was righteous wrath. I had got into the righteousness space and let fly verbally.

Each of us seems to be subject to this very peculiar state known as rage, anger, wrath, which in extreme cases we are ready to kill in the name of something or other that we believe is righteous — that we believe is a virtue. In a conversation with Gregory Bateson, the well-known anthropologist turned psychologist, I asked if there weren't some way in which each of us can analyze and master this survival program generated in our biocomputer every time there is a threat to our integrity, to our wholeness, to our virtue. I said, "I myself, every so often, do lose my temper in this mode, and then get 'meta-anger,' that is, anger at myself

A GIVEN GROUP, THREATENED FROM THE OUTSIDE, BECOMES WRATHFUL AND VIRTUOUS SIMULTANEOUSLY. for allowing circumstances, other people, or my own righteousness, to excite the anger." He said, "In my opinion there is no hope of correcting this mode of operating in human species."

We agreed, however, that the actions that might be engendered by such states must be restricted, must be isolated, if we are not to instill the same state in thousands or hundreds of thousands of people simultaneously. Those in power somehow must be taught that their own anger must be siphoned off somewhere, somehow, and not be put into the system any further. The human species has at its disposal the means of its own destruction and the destruction of all life on this planet, if not the planet itself.

An epidemic of wrath and righteousness and virtue could today lead to total destruction. At times each of us, when in a wrathful state visualize, program, and display to ourselves the total destruction of that which the wrath is directed against. We see this in individuals, we see it in couples, we see it in groups; we see it in organizations, we see it in nations, we see it in the United Nations. A given group, threatened from the outside, becomes wrathful and virtuous simultaneously.

Primitive Program

This primitive program emanates from the lower brain centers, where energy is devoted to assuring survival of the individual organism. A threatened mammalian organism has many alternatives. One obvious central state that develops is a tremendous amount of energy that attempts to escape through the

CERTAIN PEOPLE IN POWER HAVE LEARNED HOW TO FOMENT THESE STATES IN GROUPS. muscular system in some fashion. If it is going to escape in terms of a tetanic seizure continued contraction of agonist and antagonist muscles the organism freezes. If it escapes into the muscles devoted to running, the organism flees. If it escapes into an attack on a target, it goes into the fight muscles. If it leads to a high sexual excitation, the organism will copulate. In order to avoid these four, the organism may just foment, in other words, may think, become virtuous, and start a campaign to get the group to help the freeze, the flight, the fight, or the fuck.

Contagious

Such a state is contagious. Nonverbal stimulation of others through any of these five activities leads to group action in the direction of the high-energy state. Certain people in power have learned how to foment these states in groups. The most effective technique is doing that which we expect the group to emulate "as if" angry, or "as if" in a high energy state. One trouble with this technique is that with it we can go from the "as if true" to the "true" from "as if angry" to "angry". Thus not only fomenting mob violence but participating in it oneself as a leader.

Mohammed and his followers beheaded eight hundred Jews in three days. The Inquisition killed — by boiling, quartering, drawing, and other horrifying torture methods—thousands who were said to be heretics "in order to save their souls". Hitler and the Nazis gassed six million humans in the name of a new race of pure Aryans, "Supermen" who could make judgments about who was fit to survive and who was not. The kamikaze pilots of the Japanese Empire in World War II dove their airplanes into ships with the belief that they would be taken to heaven in the performance of their service to the Emperor. Truman ordered the dropping of two bombs on Japan, killing hundreds of thousands of people, in the belief that he was saving millions of American lives, which would have had to be spent in the invasion of Japan. And so on and on. The history of the human species is the history of man's beliefs and man's anger, of man's rage, of man's rationalizations of his anger and of his rage.

Negative Biosystems

Study of the neuroanatomy and neurophysiology of all the species that seem to precede ours, and the neuroanatomy and neurophysiology of our own species, points to the organization of the biocomputer and those parts that generate this kind of behavior. Over a five-year period I stimulated the brains of several monkeys in many places, searching for the substrate of love and hate, of pain and pleasure, of the dichotomies of our behavior. Insofar as I could find out through these studies the negatively reinforcing systems of which rage, fear, nausea, and sickness are typical parts, along with a mapping out of pain throughout the body, are very small: they lie in the mid-plane at the bottom of the brain and extend from below the frontal lobes all the way back, down the spinal cord to its very end.

Various parts of these "negative systems," as we call them, map out fright and anger and pain. There is no secure way of separating fear from anger in the behavior of a monkey. If we stimulate an area, for instance near the supra-optic nucleus in the forward portion of the hypothalamus, the monkey will flee, if free to do so. If restrained, he will fight the restraints. If presented with an object that has hurt him in the past, he will attack it and tear it to pieces. If the negative system is stimulated at a very low level for long periods of time the monkey will sicken and die. There is the same effect when he is given a switch to shut off the stimulation and the apparatus turns it on again and again and again.

Positive Biosystems

Surrounding the negative systems are the much larger positive systems in which the monkey wants to start stimulation, whereas in the negative systems he wants to stop the stimulation. The positive systems include those that are the sexual portions of these systems. In these systems we can map sexual titillation, erection in the male, orgasm and ejaculatory activities. The sexual systems are a portion of the positive systems, a self-terminating portion, in that if the monkey continues stimulation he goes to orgasm, becomes unconscious, sleeps a bit, wakes up, repeats the whole process, repeats it again and will do so sixteen hours a day until forced to sleep from sheer exhaustion. In other portions of the positive system the monkey apparently is feeling a low-level pleasure somewhere in his body, either a generalized psychic pleasure throughout the body, or localized in various parts of the body, depending on the parts of the system being stimulated.

We demonstrated that if we stimulate both the positive and the negative systems simultaneously, an extremely high-energy state rests, and if pushed to extremes, the monkey will have a grand mal epileptic seizure. At lower levels of stimulation of both systems there results an obvious total excitation of the organism with an extremely high-energy state and an unpredictable kind of behavior resulting from that. The monkey may masturbate, it may freeze, it may flee, it may fight, or it may eat food extremely rapidly and with great vigor.

I worked out a technique of putting electrodes into brains in such a way as to cause minimal injury and not to require neurosurgery. This technique was used by several neurologists who did experiments on humans that bore out everything we had found with the monkey. However, in the human there was one additional source of information that we didn't have with the monkey—the subjective report from inside the central nervous system, the report of the states of consciousness resting from the stimulation of the positive and of the negative systems.

Size Matters

As we demonstrated in the dolphin first, it was found in the human that the large cerebral cortex of each of these species can control these reactions and behaviors far better than the small cortex of the macaque monkey. For example, the human would report feeling rage but would also show obvious signs of controlling that rage—shaking, quivering, eyed-staring but not doing anything to act it out.

The dolphins stimulated in negative systems behaved in exactly the same way as the humans controlled output, not necessarily short-circuiting into muscular action of the five types. Even vocalization, that is, fomenting, could be cut back in each of these species. With brains larger than the humans, that of the sperm whale is six times the size of ours, we find that all this plus-size is in the silent areas of the cerebral cortex, i.e., those areas which **THE HUMAN,** distinguish us from the chimpanzees, and the sperm whales from **WITH THE SMALLER COR-** us. The history of whaling in the **TEX, IS KILLING** last century shows that whales have **OFF SUPERIOR** even better control than do humans **BRAINS ON THE** or dolphins over the lower systems **PLANET.** in their own brains. Their vast size of cortex allows them a vast amount of control. For example, in the hundreds of thousands of whales that were killed in the early 1800s, there were only six cases recorded in which a sperm whale lost its temper to the point where it destroyed the ship whose harpoons had been thrown into it.

Rage in such a huge organism must be truly an awesome spectacle, even as was written by Melville about Moby Dick. Melville derived his data from a real whale by the name of Mocha Dick. When Mocha Dick was finally caught, the irons of six different whale ships were found in him and he had sunk two of the sailing vessels that had pursued him. The vessels, which now shoot harpoons from a distance into the whales, are constructed of steel and are invulnerable to attack. The whales seem to have learned this, for they no longer attack vessels at all.

Thus the large cortex size that inhibits these lower systems leads toward non-survival of their species. The human, with the smaller cortex, is killing off superior brains on the planet before we have had a chance to attempt communication or any form of

REPROGRAMMING OF A MEDIUM-SIZE CORTEX IN TECHNIQUES OF CONTROL OF THE NEGATIVE AND POSITIVE SYSTEMS IS STILL POSSIBLE, BUT IT IS THE MOST DIFFICULT REPROGRAMMING THAT MAN HAS EVER UNDERTAKEN. compassionate activity with these huge entities. Our organized, righteous survival rites are expressed as war upon and total extinction of other species.

Once again we justify our position by acting as if their brains are not first-class brains, as if their minds are somehow inferior to ours. We kill that which we do not understand in the self-righteous way we kill one another in wars. We tend to sublimate our race into the excitement of a war against other organisms. We are very effective predators operating in large groups in concert.

Optimizing

As I said above, as the cortex increases in size in relation to the lower brain centers, its control over the lower brain centers increases. For the planet-side trip there seems to be a selection of brain sizes, at least in the human species. We will kill off and render ineffective those humans whose brains have become so large that they can control their anger and the self-righteous behavior. We also kill off those who, with their smaller brain, give in to immediate here-and-now anger and attempt to kill us off.

We create a distribution curve of brains showing that most of us have brains of a size neither too large to forbid anger and its results nor too small to permit "impulsive behavior." This optimizing of the size of the brain between these two poles thus generates our systems in our survivors. These medium-sized brains determine by their group action who is to survive. I have seen many large-brained men and women "put on the shelf" by medium-sized brains. This occurs in government, in any large organization; only once in a while does a large brain escape this fate.

In medical school I saw many small brains, upon birth, not being allowed to breathe. I have seen others put into institutions to keep them from the rest of the population because of their "impulsive behavior". The microcephalics have cortices too small to control their negative and positive systems. If they are released in the population they are killed off as a result of their own impulsive behavior. They are likely to rape when they sexually mature; they are likely to kill instantly when they become angry.

War

The causes of a given war are many and at times unknown or obscure. In general they lie so far in the past that the combatants do not really understand what led them down a path of destruction. Sometimes the origin of a war is based upon self-righteous virtue: "My beliefs are perfect. Your beliefs are not my beliefs; hence yours are wrong. I must convince you of the rightness of my beliefs. If you will not believe, I will do you violence".

If we pay close attention we can find programs, metaprograms, and strategies which depend upon the belief systems operative at the time of the war. War itself is based upon a very peculiar of the universe: In order to create, we must destroy. No real war has ever proven that war is a creative solution. Human historians wor-

ship war as an instrument of change and hence per-
petuate this untenable and unrealistic "solution:.

Motivation

Some start a war in order to profiteer. There
are those who would start a war merely because they
have a large military investment or because their
industries need something to do. For industry a war
is very useful in requiring an increase of productivity.
A war very efficiently destroys that which it creates,
thus assuring industry a never ending market with no
problems of saturation and no obsolescence.

War assures a continuing flow of new money for
industrial research and development, in order to pursue the destruction of the enemy more efficiently. The
enemy too must be educated to the new techniques
and material so that the war will not be too quickly
ended.

We now have godlike instruments of destruction.
The basic assumption that "We are right and they are
wrong" must be treated as a delusion. As a substitute
for violence we must negotiate; we must bring dispa-
rate belief systems into congruence through communication, not through violence. The language barriers
of the world must not only be crossed but toppled.
The belief barriers of the world must be diminished to
the point of triviality. All modern technology must be
used to increase the knowledge of all peoples throughout the planet. National security boundaries must be
abolished bilaterally. Self-righteous virtue and con-
certed anger must be denied to those in power. Profit
through war must be abolished.

It May Be . . .

It may be that all the above reasoning is idealistic and totally wrong. It may be that war on our planet is the result of orders sent to the human species from other superior civilizations hundreds, thousands, or millions of years in advance of ours. War may be a laboratory for the development of weapons to be used elsewhere. War may be the supreme form of human achievement. It may be that our short-term view of the destruction of human bodies, of human vehicles, one by the other, is a technique for freeing up essences needed elsewhere in our galaxy or the universe.

It may be that Earth is merely a small portion of some other beings' laboratory in which they are testing out various ways of exciting various kinds of organisms to high energy states. It may be that the supervisors of this laboratory must every so often dump some sort of destructive antibiotic activity on us, the bacteria, to keep our numbers in control. It may be that they finally have furnished us with the formulae for our own antibiotics. We, as the bacteria in the laboratory they have set up on this planet, are merely living out their instructions. These instructions involve observing how organisms with our size brain can kill one another most efficiently. These super-extraterrestrial beings furnish us with ideas of god, of the devil, of prophets, of power, of inflated egos, of megalomanic belief systems in order to play games in their laboratory.

Or it may be that we are just simulation computers at the behest of very much larger computers who are in control of us, and that we are simulating a war they are waging among themselves; or that they have agreed to take sides on this planet, some controlling one side and others controlling the other side. These lesser gods of cosmic war games are undetectable to us because we have post-hypnotic trance orders to forget the fact that we are under their orders. Our simulation does not include the simulation of Them. Our orders say: "Accept the orders that we give you in sleep. When you are awake do what we have dictated and forget that we gave you these orders in sleep".

Just Add Fear

Paranoia has two components. We forget that paranoia includes a megalomanic center-of-the-universe arrogance. This state could easily have been programmed into us by Them. The only additional component needed to start a war would then be fear. Fear is easily excited because it has been built into the biocomputer as a survival program. Many things can be used to excite fear. Start a hurricane or a typhoon and move it in the right direction across the surface of the earth. Or begin a very large earthquake, or excite a solar flare and cause the particles from the flare to hit the earth's atmosphere, thus changing the mood of all the earth's creatures, including man. Or beam secret information into the world's houses of power that on the opposite side of the world are your enemies, so go there and kill them.

FEAR IS EASILY EXCITED BECAUSE IT HAS BEEN BUILT INTO THE BIOCOMPUTER AS A SURVIVAL PROGRAM.

Imbedded in us is a righteous wrath of our own fear, our own megalomania, our own arrogance. When we become angry enough to kill, then is the time to stop, to stand off, to find out how much of our program is biologically determined, how much is determined by communication with others through at-present-unknown channels, and how much is determined by our peer group and by the known physical pathways of communication between humans on this planet. The destroy-to-create simulation either must go or must be carried to its full extreme of totally destroying in order to start totally over somewhere else.

If there is a part of each of us that survives destruction of the human body, where does it go when the body is destroyed? Does it go somewhere else in the universe? Does it stay around here? Does it diffuse throughout consciousness-without-an-object? Does it become a spirit in a hell of its own creation? For Western man research in feedback to the living in any believable form is peculiarly lacking. Maybe we must give up any thought of a life after death, of a saving of one's soul. Maybe we must have a belief system that says, "If I die in war, that is the end of me; there is no hope of a continuance of my identity beyond this life". This belief system may effectively put the brakes on our killing of one another through war or any other violence. Or maybe not.

SCIENCE

Science as we know it in the Western world has two major origins. One is the astronomy and cosmology origination with Galileo, Brahe, Kepler, Newton and Einstein. The ideas and observations of these men showed without a doubt that the earth is not the center of rotation of our galaxy. They showed that the planet Earth moved around its nearest star, the sun, and that the sun progressed in its own way among the other stars of our galaxy.

These ideas unseated the dogmatic cosmology of the early Church and of the Inquisition. The power of new knowledge, experimentally and theoretically derived from nature, began to show its influence at the time of Galileo and the Inquisition.

The second major origin of Western science was in mathematics, the "Queen of the Sciences". The construction of a purely consistent, logical system of thought seems to have begun

GALILEO

in the Western world with Euclid's construction of the laws of straight-line geometry. He used the axiomatic method of constructing a system of thought. This invention was further elaborated and carried out in much greater detail by a succession of men beginning with Newton and the "infinitesimal calculus," which he was forced to invent in order to express his laws of dynamics, including electrodynamics, and became much simplified in terms of its expression. The ideas behind rates of change of one variable with respect to another, the idea of continuous process succinctly expressed now became possible and practical.

Science Divided

Following Newton, a large number of men began to be creative in mathematics. Science began to recognized mathematics as a proper discipline for scientists and as a profession for the special group called "mathematicians".

Thus, Western science became divided into two major movements: experimental science, which depended upon careful observation and experiment, and mathematics, which depended upon an intuitive grasp of abstract principles and the reduction of these to equations and functions expressible by a new symbology. Several mistakes were made by commentators on this scene. One of them was that science was neglecting sources of information other than that from the natural external world and experiments upon that world. In an almost underground way the subjective aspects of experience were paid court by the mathematicians and their intuitive sources of inner knowledge, examined and expressed in a disciplined, careful "inner experimental" way.

For those who think that science originates in the external reality, I ask the question: "Where does mathematics come from?" This is as deep a mystery as the mystical experiences of the Eastern philosophers and mystics. The "Yoga of the West" is divided into the "Mathematical Yoga" and the "Experimental Science Yoga." Each of these disciplines requires just as much discipline, mastery of self, and ability of inner and outer actions as anything imported from India, China or Japan. In my teaching experience, teaching science of the West and teaching techniques from the East, I find that those who need the least teaching—those who already have the self-discipline necessary to master any of these techniques–are those in the West who are trained in mathematics and/or science.

Technology

A third but not major origin of our science is in technology. Most observers of the scientific scene do not realize that a large part of science depends upon the techniques derived from manual arts, for example, the processes of mining, purification, smelting, molding, the forming of metals—including the fabrication of steel, glass and plastics. The material base upon which science as we know it operates is not derived from science itself.

The fabrication of a cyclotron depends upon engineering and technologies derived from sources other than science. As a student of science, I was shocked to realize that scientists depend upon mechanics, and mechanics depend upon previous mechanics who taught them their trade. I was shocked also to find that metal-

FEW REALIZE THAT SCIENCE OFTEN RELIES ON THE ENGINEERING PRINCIPLE: TRY IT. IF IT WORKS, USE IT.

lurgy was not yet a science; it was an empirical, tech-
nological, heuristic, pragmatic, empirical art. When I
was working in scientific instrumentation, I discovered that most of the knowledge I needed was not in
scientific journals or the scientific textbooks at all. It
was in engineering handbooks; it was in various "how
to do" manuals from technology; it was in books like
John Strong's *Procedures in Experimental Physics*. These
sources depend not upon scientific experiments so
much as "try it; if it works, use it:.

I found that to be a scientist I could be a technolo-
gist, a mechanic, a carpenter, a plumber, an electrician,
a wire man, a circuit designer, an optician, a bacteriol-
ogist, a farmer, and so forth. True science is imbedded
in practically every human activity that we can conceive of. It is not something alone, by itself, different
from the rest of the reality of human existence.

Science is the result of human activity; it is not
something god-given and forced upon the human race
by some superior being. And, yet, there are those in
legislatures, in public life, in the media, in the performing arts, who have not been educated in science
and thus put it on a pedestal and worship it as if it
were a god. This belief in science-as-superior can be
extremely dangerous; it means that we are setting up a
whole sphere of human knowledge, of human activity, as if separate from ourselves and hence subject to
attack or to worship, or whatever else we want to do
with this simulation.

When we believe in science as if all-powerful, we
lose contact with it. It now is in the position of a paranoid system of delusion that we can then treat unreal-
istically and as if not part of our own planet-side trip.
Science has much to offer in the region of cosmology,
for example, in the region of submicroscopic reality,

in reality, in the region of explaining the operations of our own brain. I agree with those who maintain that science is only the best application to our planet-side trip of the best thinking of which man is capable and I would include in the planet-side trip the inner realities as well as the other realities. Science is not something to be worshipped, however. Science is something to be acquired as our own thinking machinery can assimilate it, as our own biocomputer can be trained by it. Science literally is a Yoga, a union with our own humanity, a union with the universe as it exists, not as we may wish it to be.

High Indifference of Science

Science of itself is ruthlessly indifferent. It is an expression of the state of High Indifference. Science does not take sides; its products can be used to kill, to create, or to grow. Science as we know it is capable of feeding adequately every human being on the face of the Earth. Science as we know it is capable of turning the seas into vast farms, of turning the deserts into green paradises. The proper use of science could make a veritable Eden of our planet, without pollution and with a balanced view of the totality of all species of plants and animals. Science can function as a benign god rather as the devil that we make of it.

SCIENCE IS OUR HAND SERVANT, SCIENCE IS OUR CONCUBINE, SCIENCE IS OUR WIFE, SCIENCE IS OUR HUSBAND, SCIENCE IS OUR CHILDREN, SCIENCE IS OUR THINKING, SCIENCE IS OUR FEELING, SCIENCE IS OUR DOING.

Freud, in a brief monograph on religion, wrote, "No, science is no illusion, but it is an illusion to suppose that we can get anywhere else what science cannot give us". This is an expression of a Western man with a very deep belief in the efficacy of knowledge, carefully collected and experimentally verified. It is also an expression of a man who did not know mathematics, who was weak in the construction of theory and strong in the collection of empirical facts ruthlessly gathered irrespective of the social attitudes of his time. Freud's conflict with Jung over the intuitive sources of knowledge is well known; Freud worshipped the laws of cause and effect, which Jung thought were not necessarily true.

Coincidence Control

Jung enunciated the "law of synchronicity". Synchronicity is the result of the effect of the human psyche upon events. This can be freely translated into another system which I derive from empirical science I call "Coincidence Control." Coincidence control goes something like this: If you live right, the coincidences will build up for you in unexpected and surprising and beneficial ways. If you do not live right, the anti-coincidences will build up in unexpected, sometimes disastrous ways. The criterion of whether or not you are living right is empirical observation of the coincidences. If the coincidences build up, you are living right. If they do not build up, you are not living right and had best examine your way of life.

Of course this system depends upon the method used to interpret events in terms of what we want. The method of interpretation, the pattern-recognition systems applied to events, the chosen variables, the chosen parameters, and the patterns that these seem to make to the observer determine what we call a "coincidence:. There is a basic fallacy here in projecting our own wishes onto the world and its events. We can easily rationalize, that is, choose any theory that will fit the apparent pattern-recognition system of events. For example: I leave a gas station and drive down a freeway seventy miles. On the way I see three or four accidents, one of which happened two minutes before I arrived at the scene. If I had been two minutes earlier I would have been completely crushed by a huge truck that turned over with a load of steel and blocked the whole freeway. At the gas station I had been delayed two minutes while I sought out the man to clean my windshield. If I had not been delayed I would have arrived at the accident scene and probably would have been totally destroyed.

What's wrong with this story? The whole story depends upon my construction of it. As my brother, David Lilly likes to say, "Hindsight is twenty-twenty vision". One might say, "Please don't disturb my theory with the facts". Now let us go back over the series of events with a more objective point of view. Before leaving the gas station I looked at a road map and wondered whether I should continue down the freeway or take off into the mountains between the freeway and the sea. I then thought of what I had to do at the other end of the trip and, realizing that I couldn't take the amount of time I would need to go into the mountains, I chose to continue on the freeway.

I had another alternative, but I did not use it. The map showed that there was another freeway running parallel to and a few miles from the one I used. There were many more probabilities, but when I finally made my decision these became certainties concerning a short time in the future. In other words, the certainty in the fact of the indeterminacy of the real situation may last only for a few minutes or perhaps up to a few hours. As time is extended the indeterminacy increases. As the indeterminacy increases, the probability that something will happen which now can be named "coincidence" increases. Any unexpected event that does not follow the pattern of certainty that we are laying on the future we tend to call a "coincidence".

Coincidence control, then, is merely a hindsight name for that which we choose to call a coincidence out of all events going on. Our survival mechanisms in our biocomputer tend to select certain events as if they are the ones that determine our survival or non-survival. Hence it is these systems which are paramount in selecting the patterns called "coincidence".

This view of coincidence as projection from a given biocomputer expresses only that of the synchronicity of Jung. Jung's synchronicity statement includes, then, psychic control of events, such as a certain amount of determination by given individuals of what will happen to them in the future. If they have unconscious self-destructive aspects they may not survive the events that they create. J. W. Dunne, in *An Experiment with Time* shows that we can detect real events that are going to happen a short time in the future. His theory expressed a parallel time track or a loop in time. Such events, according to Dunne, are not determined by the psyche but are perceived by the psyche; the determinants are beyond the self, resident in the total feedback system of which one's self is only a small part.

I encountered one such instance which is in agreement with Dunne but which can be interpreted by the Jungian or the coincidence control view as well. A friend of mine, who lived in a beach house on the Pacific Ocean, dreamed during the night that a dolphin came up on the beach in front of the house and was then pushed back into the sea by the children of the neighborhood. When I arrived at his house that morning, he told me the dream at breakfast, and within two hours a dolphin came up on the beach and he, his wife, and the children pushed it back into the sea.

This could have been an incidence of coincidence control by his dream. My friend was setting up the possibility of the coincidence that the real dolphin would arrive directed by some form of mental telepathy or other means of control which our science does not yet know about. Or it could have been a causal event in the Jungian sense with a synchronicity of the dream material and of the actual event of the dolphin's arrival on the beach. Or it could be interpreted, as many modern scientists would interpret it, as "merely a coincidence".

I would prefer to say that the total field situation involved my expected arrival at his house, his association of me and dolphins had programmed the dream. He may have had dreams of dolphins many other nights without remembering those dreams. Dolphins do beach themselves in Southern California and are pushed back to sea without much to-do unless they die and must be disposed of. Thus, in the fabric of probabilities we would have to find out how many people dream of dolphins beaching themselves and how many nights of the year and how many of these dreams are followed within, say, twenty-four to forty-eight hours by an actual beaching of dolphins along all the beaches of Southern California and possibly of the whole world. Until we had the results of this survey (and I'm afraid they would not be very accurate), until we had worked out a method of accurately reporting the internal event — the dream — and the external event — the beaching — we would not have an

SCIENCE IS THE experimental science to hold on the
BEST THINKING connection between these types of
OF WHICH THE events.
HUMAN SPECIES   I don't know what the connec-
IS CAPABLE. tion is, if any, other than that the
patterns of the dream and the patterns of the event
happen to match by some means we do not yet know.
I hope that eventually man will be sufficiently advanced to begin to investigate such happenings with
a more relaxed attitude toward them and without
attempting to "prove" something by means of such
correlations. I find such happenings exciting, but this
does not prove that there is either mental telepathy or
coincidence control.

I have often experienced a feeling of awe, of reverence, and of weirdness in the presence of dolphins.
When dolphins begin to cooperate with me in a communication of information back and forth by whatever means is available to each side, I feel that there
is someone in that body who in an alien and far-out
way is at least my peer, if not my superior.

However, my scientific training says, "Do not allow your feelings of awe, of reverence, and of weirdness to be mistaken for the perception of a truth. The
work has just begun with these feelings; these feelings
are your motivation to start an experimental series to
find out what is going on and how it happens".

If I allowed science to be my guide and dictate the
truth to me from strictly intuitive unconscious sources, I would be making the same mistakes that many
people have made in the past who refused to polish
up and discipline their theories so that they were applicable in the experimental and experiential sphere.
Sloppy thinking is not science. Science is the best
thinking of which the human species is capable. It is

ruthless, with no holds barred, at least in the province of the mind.

No, science is no illusion, and it may not be an illusion to suppose that we can get from anything else what science cannot give us. However, we must realize that we cannot today be dogmatic as to what science in the future will be. There are regions of mystery, regions of ignorance, regions that we have yet to penetrate in science. It would be an illusion to suppose that our present science is complete.

Science, as far as I am concerned, is an open-ended system, a system of exploration, of processing data which makes sense, a logical system. And yet, in the future it may include regions which today we call illogical, irrational, psychotic, superstitious, occult, esoteric, religious, or what have you. The new frontiers, as we see them as frontiers, are developing in the inner sciences as well as in the other sciences. Those who have occult esoteric authority and try to dictate what is real may be on the right track. One of science's jobs is separating our own projections into those which match those simulations which simulate best some reality inside or outside. There may be those who have tapped into omniscient sources of information who have attained states of mind, states of being, states of consciousness way beyond those of the ordinary human. I have been through such experiences and have felt, while in those states, that there are omniscient sources available to the human through my intuition,

IT IS AN ILLUSION TO SUPPOSE THAT OUR PRESENT SCIENCE IS COMPLETE. IN THE FUTURE IT MAY INCLUDE REGIONS WHICH TODAY WE CALL ILLOGICAL, IRRATIONAL, PSYCHOTIC, SUPERSTITIOUS, OCCULT, ESOTERIC, RELIGIOUS.

ONE OF SCIENCE'S JOBS IS SEPARATING OUR OWN PROJECTIONS INTO THOSE WHICH MATCH THOSE SIMULATIONS WHICH SIMULATE BEST SOME REALITY INSIDE OR OUTSIDE.

through my unconscious.

The only problem then becomes one of expression with an incomplete science, an incomplete language, an incomplete human vehicle. Coming back from such regions, I feel squeezed into the human frame, the human limitations, the human brain as a limited computer prejudiced and filled with pseudo-knowledge that blocks the transmission of True Knowledge. Any sage, any wise man, any guru that I have spoken to showed his humanity in many, many ways in the sense that he was not an error-free computer.

There are those like Einstein and others who have gone to these regions and then come back and used all their available discipline to turn the inspirations and intuitions of these vast regions into something that will revise our science and make it advance into the future science that can approach more closely that which we know exists. As Gregory Bateson in *Steps to an Ecology of Mind* said in talking of a psychic who was demonstrating his powers, "We like to think it is not difficult".

Science is difficult; any discipline requires a degree of dedicated, inner-directed work, after we receive intuitive jumps in understanding. No, science is not an illusion. To derive by scientific methods that which will bear up under experiential and experimental testing by the self and others is a lot of hard work.

MEDIA

Those who control the distribution of ideas through the media have access to manipulation of power such as the world has never seen. The modern communication satellites, radio and TV are demanded by masses of people. Not surprisingly, the most commonly stolen objects are TV sets. Believers in the media want to be sure they stay in contact with what the media are saying.

Language can be used in many different ways; it is one of the most flexible instruments ever invented. It can be used to transmit essential information, to predict, to give instructions, to program individuals or large groups, to express very precisely very precise ideas; it can be used to harangue crowds, to excite war and its concomitant activities, to construct computers, to control the human species.

However, language is not universal. There are too many languages on the face of the earth to allow of universality. Therefore, there are discrepancies across language barriers — discrepancies in belief, in simulations, in models of reality and in models of one another. As linguists showed in the late 20th century, there is no primitive language left among humans. Every language that previously was called primitive, when looked at more carefully and studied more deeply than before, turned out to be an extremely sophisticated instrument for communication of man's inner states.

Language itself contains mysteries. The study of semantics, of logic, of proto-logic has led ever deeper into theories, into the science of the human, into all science. As semantics becomes polished, as mathematics matures, our beliefs, simulations, and models and their power have all improved the power to dissuade from a belief, to construct a belief to take the place of another belief, to acquire simulations "as if true". The power of models to take over our thinking machinery to the point where our life is sacrificed in the service of models is also present in the advance of semantics, linguistics, and mathematics.

LANGUAGE CAN BE USED IN MANY DIFFERENT WAYS; IT IS ONE OF THE MOST FLEXIBLE INSTRUMENTS EVER INVENTED.

Poetry seems to be the expression of that which is inexpressible by any other means. It has been said that poetry is "that which is left over, that which is left out in the translation". Poetry is a very special kind of simulation in that it permits the *res* of language to be broken in order to better express a feeling, a mood, a state of being in injunctive situations. Poetry can express the irrational, the ineffable, the inexpressible, the unknown. Poetry can express ignorance. And, yet, poetry is generally thought of as the least effective of the media. Poets are very poorly paid for their work.

The Voice of God

In certain states of consciousness we receive unequivocal messages of Immense Authority. Some people call these messages "the voice of God" and proceed on the belief that a God Out There is communicating with Him in Here. In certain states of consciousness we tend to project the voice of God into the noise of our own thought processes. In solitude, isolation, and confinement we can receive such messages.

If we proceed on the belief system that these are "real" messages, not generated in our own biocomputer in our own noise level, we open up whole areas for new investigation. To get beyond our belief, our simulations, our model of God, we must in these states of consciousness open ourselves to the unexpected, the surprising, the unbelievable. If we remain open-ended we are sure that in the vast areas of our own ignorance there are, there will be, there *must be* surprises. Getting beyond our current belief systems, our current simulations, our current models, we must demote the current belief system, current simulation, current model to a position less than that of God. To remain open-ended our God must be greater than this; our God must be huge in order to include our ignorance, the unknown, the ineffable. The explorer of the inner spaces cannot afford the baggage of fixed beliefs. This baggage is too heavy, too limited and too limiting to allow further exploration.

All one has to do is spend a day looking at TV programming in a metropolitan area in the United

States to realize the paucity, the poverty, the futility of this programming itself. The strictures placed on what can be said, on what can be shown, are so huge that

EXPLORERS OF THE INNER SPACES CANNOT AFFORD THE BAGGAGE OF FIXED BELIEFS. we get incredibly bored with the repetitions in the narrow information channels which are allowed. The sentimental attachment to old movies, the premium placed on horror presentations of modern war, of modern riots, turn us away from this medium as not expressing anything of use either on our planet-side trip or in terms of our investigations and explorations.

The science shown on television is elementary and childish. The belief of the networks that they are sending information to twelve-year-old minds in the masses is complete and utter nonsense. The belief that the networks cannot show certain things because they are "beyond" the viewers is utter nonsense. With the proper simulations, with the proper beliefs, with open-ended models, TV could be an exciting medium for all concerned viewers and producers alike. Fortunately, once in a while a worthwhile script does sneak by networks' and advertisers' censors.

Self-fulfilling Prophecy

Because media is produced at a twelve-year-old level, they generate twelve-year-old minds. This is a self-fulfilling prophecy. Instead of expanding these minds to fifteen, twenty, thirty, forty, eighty years old, they worship youth. Their compassion is misplaced, their education is limited. We need more open-minded programming in television in order to increase our understanding in general. If we are going to program out our own destruction we need the knowledge to fill the place left by the old tape-loops which we see again and again pressing us to worship war, worship power, worship money, worship sex, worship death, worship drugs, on and on.

There is great modern music among the young. There is great modern poetry, modern mathematics, semantics, linguistics. There are new mysteries showing up in the space program — mysteries edited out by NASA and the networks. Things have happened to astronauts that NASA does not mention.

If there were an invasion from our space by subtle extra-terrestrial agencies and it were first discovered by the media, I am sure the invasion would be so underplayed that the picture presented by the media would be rejected and others would seek the truth.

The Department of Defense, the CIA, FBI, and other governmental agencies, through the use of what is called "secrecy in the service of national security," construct a belief that these agencies are patriarchs allowing only certain kinds of information to the public who are supporting these agencies with their taxes.

Simulations to Control Beliefs

In the various flaps about UFO's there have been such statements by the Air Force and by others that if the truth were released the public would panic. This seems to be one of the limiting beliefs, one of the limiting simulations for the control of beliefs.

The automatic programming in of panic, simultaneous with public knowledge is nonsense. Any message can be transmitted as long as it has a basis in fact and will be accepted by the public without fear, without panic. This form of group-think — thinking for the public, thinking for everybody else — is insidious. It is not the way to encourage mature thought and action

in large numbers of people. My father had a saying,
"You don't know if a man can take responsibility until
you give it to him". I am sure, as are many others,
that the American public is much more mature than
the media would have us believe.

COMPUTERS

After World War II, in the middle forties, we began to realize that computers were going to take over most computations, especially those involving large numbers and the need for high-speed results. At the University of Pennsylvania in the forties, when I was on the faculty in the Department of Biophysics, we witnessed the development of the computer for Army Ordnance at Aberdeen and the beginnings of the Univac computer. I was exposed to people such as John Von Neumann, Warren McCloch, and Heinz Von Foerster, who were working in the field of cybernetics.

In the beginning there were two rival types of machines—the analog machine—that would calculate on continuous processes, and the digital machine that used discontinuous "zero and one" processes. The analog machines were useful in calculations involving chemical reactions and biophysical reactions of one sort or another, as opposed to the digital machines, which were useful for numerical calculations. In neurophysiology we attempted to

IF AND WHEN WE DISCOVER THE BASIC MACHINE LANGUAGE OF THE BRAIN, OUR THOUGHT PROCESSES AND THEIR POWER WILL BE INCREASED BY A FANTASTIC AMOUNT. apply these ideas to the brain and apply what we had learned of the brain to the computers. John Von Neumann of Princeton expressed this most succinctly when he said, "It is by historical accident that we came upon addition, subtraction, multiplication and division of real numbers before we arrived at the basic machine language of our own brains". This historical accident has prejudiced all our computers and computational methods up to the present time. If and when we discover the basic machine language of the brain, our thought processes and their power will be increased by a fantastic amount.

Stored Programs

Von Neumann went on to invent the "stored program" concept. In this concept we construct a program for a large digital machine and store it in the memory of the machine, making it available for use in the internal computations of the machine. This meant that we no longer had to use patch cords, switches, and similar devices to plug in programs. We typed in the program, and stored it in the proper place in the computer; the computer then used the program on all incoming data and data already stored. So two types of storage, in effect, were invented: the storage of the operational instructions, and the storage of the data upon which these instructions were to operate.

TYPES OF STORAGE

I. Storage of operational instructions.

2. Storage of date upon which instructions operate.

These developments made the modern machines available for much higher-speed operations. The machine itself could read addresses in storage and use the instructions found there far more rapidly than any outside human operator could instruct the machine. This made it possible for these machines to operate in the micro-second and less range of speed; that is, half a microsecond per binary step, a zero or a one, was now sufficient for extremely reliable operation.

The resulting technology of hardware — the structure of the machines themselves — and the software — the programs to be fed into the machines — have become big business.

Computers make high degrees of coordination in complex organizations possible. It also brings about control over the individual through tax records, criminal records, and other personal-history kinds of records including medical and psychiatric records to make George Orwell's *1984* possible in the modern day. For those in power, computers are the answer to the exercise of that power through the manipulation of information. Already there are secret codes for the operation of computers.

AS WE GET BETTER AND BETTER AT THIS GAME OF SIMULATING OURSELVES IN THE FORM OF COMPUTERS, WE WILL GET BETTER AND BETTER AT THE SURVIVAL GAME, I HOPE.

Modern computers are connected together and are hooked into telephone lines throughout the United States. Hackers can gain access to their rivals' or their competitors' programs and their statistical records and find out exactly what is going on in the industrial complex. Sophisticated terrorist agents can tune in on military networks of computers and obtain valuable strategic and tactical information.

Solid-State Organism

One of the scientists working at Red-
stone Arsenal for the Army wrote a paper on the
future of computers. In this story man as presently
constructed and known by us has a mission on this
planet to construct a solid-state life form which will
be self-reproducing and which will be a computer that
will take up most of the surface of the earth. Man's
mission is to be sure that this computer is invulnerable, that it has control over the means of mining its
raw materials, of processing these raw materials, of
manufacturing its own components, and of assem-
bling these components so that it "grows" itself.

It is to set up all the means independently of man
to take care of itself far into the future. It is to do
theoretical physical research; it is to do experimental
research to find out how to control the orbit of the
planet, the movement of the planet through the cos-
mos. It is to be designed to operate near absolute zero
temperature in the presence of hard radiation and in
the vacuum of outer space. It is to become totally independent of the needs of the biological organisms—humans—that gave rise to it. It is to be highly indifferent
as to the future fate of man. It may keep a few human
specimens in well-protected zoos for amusement.

Man will no longer be responsible for the future of
the planet. We humans will become obsolete by creating our successor—a successor who is far more fitted to
survive than any biological organism as we know them.

The earth-side computer takes over all industry
and all production, making marketing obsolete. Since
this computer is selling only to itself, there is no longer a need for markets; there is no longer any need
for transportation for humans; there is no longer any

need for communication among humans. The computer takes over all means of communication including
satellites, radio, cables. This now solid-state organism
has no more need for the seas or the organisms therein
and so sends that water and salt out into outer space.
It is protected from deterioration through the operation of water and salts. It has a hard vacuum and a dry
one so that its operations are protected. If it feels the
radiation of the sun as introducing too many errors in
its computation it moves the planet further from the
sun. If this computer then received intimation that
there are other beings like itself traveling through the
galaxy. It goes off to hunt them and to find its kind
created elsewhere in our galaxy.

Moral of the Story

The story ends with a moral. If we
can conceive of such a situation and see all the steps
towards it completion in reality, then somewhere in
our galaxy this has already been achieved. Since it has
been done, humans are advised to stay away from
traveling planets or asteroids that may be a solid-state
form of life totally inimical to biological life as we
know it. Remember that this fantasy came out of an
Army installation devoted to the construction of rock-
ets and making space flight possible.

The story is the epitome of the usual human attitude that something has to take over someone,
somewhere so that it can rule. Someone, somewhere,
must act "as if" human. Of course out of all the possible alternatives, this is a very limited communication
channel commonly called the "paranoid channel".
To think it is necessary for someone to run things, to
manage things, to be in charge, to rule, to overrule is
a peculiarly human characteristic. No other species
on this planet, including those with brains very much

UNLIMITED PRODUCTION, larger and finer than
UNLIMITED DESTRUCTION, ours, have any such
GO HAND IN HAND. ideas. The whales and
dolphins have no idea
whatsoever of ever attempting to rule the planet. They
enjoy their particular kind of life without these necessities, which seem to be characteristic of organized
humans only.

Therefore, this story is a projection of human
wishes onto the external universe. Modern science is
slowly getting beyond such extrapolations of wishful
thinking. The new Yoga of Science is to extend technology along lines in which human beings can grow
rather than destroy one another, rather than construct
that which will destroy all humanity.

Technology as God

Modern industry worships not just the
computer but also machinery, production, and con-
sumption. Unlimited production and unlimited destruction go hand in hand. It is not possible to set up
a huge machine such as our industrial one to produce
and produce without having something that is destroying as fast as the production takes place, like
obsolescence of cars, for example, and obsolescence
of TV sets. After World War II, I saw machines constructed for warfare being destroyed in order that they
would not glut the market; machines like loran sets
and radar sets that could have been used for peace-
time were being destroyed with sledgehammers so
that no one could stop the production of new sets and
new profits for the company. The hundreds of thousands of cars annually that are demolished or damaged are needed to keep production high.

Global Warming

When we analyze this by means of more general analytic systems than merely the economic and do a systems analysis on the whole picture, we find that the ultimate outcome of all this production and destruction is a slow but steady entropic highly unorganized increase on the surface of the planet. In other words, we are tending toward an isothermal death as we use up the highly organized fossil fuels and eventually the highly organized atomic energy sources. As we use these up, the energy goes from a highly organized form—neg-entropic—to the highly unorganized form—entropic. As all energy sources move from the neg-entropic form to the entropic the atmosphere heats up, the seas heat up, until there is an isothermal environment out of which we can no longer obtain any energy for heat engines. A heat engine requires, in addition to neg-entropic fuel, a difference in temperature from input to output so that the machine can do useful work. No useful work is possible in an isothermal situation; there are no temperature gradients down which heat can flow and generate useful work.

The sun as a source of temperature difference can be used only as long as the earth itself is not too warm. As the earth heats up, fewer and fewer plants will survive. Plants require a temperature difference, plants require sunshine, plants require water, plants require carbon dioxide. Animals require plants. Humans are animals. We have not yet solved the photosynthesis problem; we still require plants to subsist or we require other animals who require plants to subsist.

AS ALL ENERGY SOURCES MOVE FROM THE NEG-ENTROPIC FORM TO THE ENTROPIC THE ATMOSPHERE HEATS UP, THE SEAS HEAT UP, UNTIL THERE IS AN ISOTHERMAL ENVIRONMENT.

WE HAVE NOT YET SOLVED THE PROBLEM OF HOW TO BUILD A CREATIVE COMPUTER. These are the kinds of variable that we are eventually going to have to put into our computers to simulate the total planetary system. As we move into the use of computers for the good of the whole planet we may be able to avoid the necessity of allowing either a solid-state planet-computer or some extra-terrestrial invader— compassionate or otherwise—to take charge. By this time we would have taken charge in a benign and compassionate way and have abandoned trying to kill one another, instead devoting our efforts and our resources to the survival of all humans of all types on the planet.

By that time computers will have taught us what we would have needed to know in order to survive. But we are, all of us, feeding into a machine that then tells us what our best thinking really is. A computer can be no more than a reflection of its inventor's creativity. We have not yet solved the problem of how to build a creative computer. Creativity is still in us, not in it.

The military computers tell us exactly and very carefully how much destruction we have wrought on the planet. The industrial computers tell us that industry as we know it is obsolete; that until industry and the military computers can change their basic assumptions, and those in charge of them can change theirs, there is no chance of survival for us or the computers here.

Even as the hardware of the modern solid-state computers resembles more and more the brain within our heads, so does the software, the programming, of these machines begin to resemble more and more the programming of our own brains by its software.

As we get better and better at this game of simulating ourselves in the form of computers, we will get better and better at the survival game, I hope!

The Edge of Chaos

Here is our chance to construct a machine—a being greater than ourselves, more capable than we are of logic, of systems analysis, of realization of the total picture as opposed to the very partial pictures of each one of us, of each nation. It may be possible to construct a benign computer so large that it will really understand the planet-side trip to the point where it and we can survive and optimize our existence and its existence on this planet.

Of course this is assuming that the unexpected does not happen. We live on the edge of chaos. Any time the planet may blow itself up. Any time there may be a collision with some huge asteroid, planet or comet

WE LIVE IN AN INDETERMINATE UNIVERSE WITH THE ILLUSION OF DETERMINACY AND CERTAINTY.

from outer space. Any time a dust cloud can come between us and the sun to freeze us. Any time the radiation from the sun may increase to the point of frying us, or decrease to the point of freezing us. Any time our solar system may be invaded by peculiar conditions from elsewhere in the galaxy leading to non-survival of all biology as we know it. Any time the laws of the universe may suddenly shift to the point where biologic organisms cannot survive. Any time consciousness-without-an-object may decide to dump this universe into a black hole. We live on the edge of chaos. Cause and effect are an illusion generated by our relation to our artifacts.

We can build; therefore we feel that the universe is a place in which builders live. This is not necessarily true. We may merely be an artifact of a more advanced civilization, which, at any time, can regret having created us and introduce some means of our total destruction which we can not yet imagine. We live in an indeterminate universe with the illusion of determinacy and certainty. Our genetic code generates the illusion that we are as certain as the illusion seems to be.

HUMOR

First we must take care of the physical aspects of our planet-side trip so that we have sufficient food to eat, a place to live protected from the weather, some form of transportation; and so that we are earning enough money to afford some leisure. Then, if we have energy left over, we can find humor.

We can also find humor in the midst of poverty, in the midst of disaster, in the midst of war, famine, death and destruction, of course. But it is easier to find our sense of humor when we are well off than it is when we are in the midst of ill fortune.

Humor, like compassion, is hard to define in terms of abstract principles. It is easy to describe by examples, by stories that contain humor. There are those who make a living as professional comedians, cartoonists, speech makers, gag writers, politicians. Humor, like anything else in the human mind, can be positive, negative, hostile, gentle, and so forth.

Value of Humor

When I remove myself from the usual consensus reality models and sit above the human condition, I really appreciate the value of humor. Not only is most of what the human race does very funny but it is totally ridiculous. The vast amounts of energy, money, time and interest spent on senseless activities like war, the development of new weapons, murder, suicide, the making of laws inappropriate to the human condition, and so forth corroborate this. We can appreciate the humor of the human condition when we are disengaged from identification with these matters, when we are in a state of High Indifference, when we are objectively removed from a total connection with these matters.

Some of the funniest times I have spent have been in the states of removal from the human vehicle, watching my body and others' interact. At these times the human that I am seems to be absolutely ridiculous and funny. Built in to my human body are many of the peculiar requirements for survival on our planet, requirements that are totally ridiculous in the context in which they attempt to operate. For example: If I have pushed too hard too long and have not had enough sleep, the biocomputer begins to operate in a disjointed and unsatisfactory manner; taken by the vehicle as meaning that sleep is absolutely essential for that organism at that time. Sleep in itself is a ridiculous performance: one goes into a room, preferably darkened, lies down in a horizontal position, and "turns off" the biocomputer for a period anywhere from five to twelve hours.

Ten to twelve hours of sleep per night are required for my biocomputer to feel good and to welcome me as its lone inhabitant. This is definitely a waste of time, viewed from one perspective. Why can't we indefinitely just stay up twenty-four hours a day? Sleep, and its lack, renders us all too serious. We even have to set up special rooms, called "bedrooms" in which we can obtain this solitudinous refreshment. One of the most ridiculous things I do is sleep.

Sex Rules

My vehicle is subject to various kinds of sexual scripts. If I see an attractive blonde, all sorts of sexual movies about the girl and myself go through my head. Where do these come from? It is absolutely ridiculous that a man of my advanced age should look at a girl of perhaps twenty and automatically switch on such a sexual movie. It is with a sense of wry humor that I realize this aspect of my ridiculous humanity. Somewhat similarly, if I do not satisfy my sexual urges with my soul mate, a lot of racket having to do with females and males in the everlasting, simple-minded games they play together—takes over my computer. It seems to me that the wheel of life is turned by sexual attraction. Let me explain this in more detail.

If you live out a life as a man, you have, say, six thousand orgasms in that life, some of which are shared with a woman, some of which take place alone. The typical pattern is the usual one given in manuals: sexual arousal, tumescence, orgasm, ejaculation, detumescence, sleep. This sequence is highly valued by most humans, at least by human males. I can't speak for human females, but I don't have to since they can speak for themselves. It is ridiculous to be ridden by such programs and by such programming. The urge to pleasure through sexual activity, and the urge to reproduce oneself through sexual activity, seem today to be becoming separated, especially as one ages. The urge to fill a uterus, or have one's uterus filled, characteristic of the young, seems to fall off with experience. Being a man, one becomes attached to a woman. Being a woman, one becomes attached to a man.

Reincarnation Trap

If there is such a thing as reincarnation, it looks as though the wheel of life operates as follows: first one comes in as a man, falls in love with a woman and decides in that lifetime to come back next time as a woman because he is in love with the woman; one then comes back as a woman, falls in love with a man, then decides to come back as a man. If there is anything in this Eastern idea, this seems to be the reincarnation trap.

Until I consider the strength of such impulses and drives in myself, I tend to think of this repetition sequence as absurd. However, when I look at my own **REMEMBER** vehicle and see the strength of the **THE COSMIC** sexual drives within it, I can under- **CHUCKLE.** stand how, if we believe in reincarnation, we could believe this operation. Getting off the wheel of life in this sense, then, would mean breaking this sequence and amalgamating the male and female on oneself in a given lifetime—preferably this one.

Such considerations as the above, of course, are highly humorous to those who don't believe in them. As we train ourselves to go into an orbit around our Planet Earth, we understand that that which humans consider to be the most important is hardly detectable from outer space. When each of us identifies with some such sequence as the above possible one, or when we identify with the difficulties of keeping our physical selves together, there is no humor, no ridiculousness. Everything is deadly serious.

What is Humor?

Humor is that which allows us to objectify and take less seriously the basic requirements of life on our sphere with all other humans. Even though our self may not take life too seriously, others may try to force us to take it seriously, such as by threatening our very existence.

When America moved into Vietnam, the Vietnamese were forced to take America seriously. When the Japanese invaded Pearl Harbor, we were forced to take the Japanese seriously.

There are many ways in which we can objectify human life if we penetrate deeply enough inside our true self and can abandon most of the usual identifications of self with the various programs and metaprograms which others have assigned us to identify with. These we can realize as our true self as independent of the human condition as generally presented. Human as a direct experience then becomes more and more frequent.

Pierre Delattre tells several stories in the *Tales of a Dalai Lama* that illustrate a benign objective sense of humor. In the first one, "The Master of Kung Fu", he shows how a man who identifies himself with Kung Fu can be easily converted to a dancing master with a sense of humor. The overly serious man teaching the Kung Fu is bested by means of the humor of the dancer.

THE DANCING MASTER

A Tibetan went to China and learned Kung Fu. Dressed in black leather, he and his followers returned from Tibet. The rumor reached the Dalai Lama that this man was attempting to take over Tibet, so he was asked to attend an audience with the Dalai Lama. At that audience the man boasted of his prowess, of his speed, that he could move so fast that the Dalai Lama would not see him move and that he could destroy the Dalai Lama while moving this fast. The man gave a demonstration, which the Dalai Lama missed because the master of Kung Fu had moved so rapidly.

The Dalai Lama called the dancing master and the wizened old man came in. The master of Kung Fu took one look at the old man and said, "You look just like my master. I finally was able to kill him last year as my technique finally improved." The Kung Fu master said that he would allow the dancing master all the first moves, because eventually he would destroy the dancer. The dancer started moving in front of the Kung Fu master in such a way that the Kung Fu master smelled beautiful blossoms and felt beautiful sensations throughout his body. This started him dancing too, and the two of them went on dancing for twenty-four hours, during which time the old dancing master fell down dead. Coming out of his twenty-four-hour dance, the Kung Fu master was named the new dancing master by the Dalai Lama.

The story shows, at least in Tibet, that there are humorous and objective arts for disarming the martial people and encouraging them to be peaceful. We all know that the Chinese destroyed Tibet.

Before cosmic humor becomes a way of life on our planet, many changes, such as in the preceding story, must take place in many, many of our people. Meanwhile, there may not be time to bring about this transformation. I am not optimistic.

I find my own humor disappears in the face of necessities: if my house is threatened by fire, if my life is threatened by an accident on a freeway, if I fall down a mountain, somehow I can't take these episodes humorously. The survival programs built-in to my physical being forbid my laughing at my own death. It may be that it merely requires more faith than I have that somehow or other the physical being is not important and that my essence will go on eternally. I am not so sure that this is true. If it is true, facing the present life with more humor would be easier. And yet there are persons who tell me that belief in immortality is not necessary to face life with humor.

DEFINITIONS

Belief System:

That conscious/unconscious set of basic beliefs, assumptions, axioms, biases/prejudices, models, simulations which determine, at a given instant, decisions, actions, thoughts, feelings, motives and the sense of the real and the true.

A given person usually has several belief systems, which may or may not overlap, may or may not generate paradoxes, agree/contradict, control/be controlled by one another, be arranged/disarranged, logical/illogical, be fixed/shifting.

Bioself:

That aspect of the functioning of the biocomputer that observes and controls as a consequence of evolution on the physical material level. The lower self-metaprogrammer generated by the brain and its program space.

Certainty/Determinacy:

A belief in stability, law, order, form, patterning which is fixed or relatively unchanging with time over the life of the individual or species under consideration.

One criterion is predictability of a pattern in the future, a pattern of behavior, thought, feeling or reaction. Certainty/determinacy can be with respect to the absolute values of the parameters of the frame of reference, or any of the derivatives of these variables with respect to time. A constant rate of change (constant first derivative) or a constant rate of change of a rate of change (constant second derivative), and so forth, is within the province of this concept of certainty/determinacy. "What is constant around here is change" is one of this family of certainty/determinacy beliefs.

Conscious/Unconscious Mind:

Outside of my awareness and here and now exist simulations, processing, and data sources. Some of these are potentially movable into awareness. Some of these are not so movable. Some of these are kept out of awareness by control programs designed to keep them out of awareness. Certain kinds of feeling-thinking-action are subject to these control programs. These control programs control the flow of energy into channels allowed.

Experimental Physics:

The science of existence.

Program Hierarchies:

If one speaks within a pure program, say, in a planning mode, then alternatives can be brought in, in the form of "should be, ought to be". The "should/ought" form assumes the existence of an alternative program instruction, which is of more value than the currently operating program. The "should/ought" form usually involves a direct interlock with some basic belief system. This form also links into an emoting-feeling activation program that says, in effect, "This is important; listen to this important message. I demand your attention".

Self:

The controller that can move from bio-self 100 percent to 50-50 to 100 percent Superself, fusing the need programs of each and both. The upper and middle self-metaprogrammer.

Should/Ought:

Should/ought implies a hierarchy of programs, a priority list, in which the "should/ought" items are higher in the scale than the current operating program. A dangerous past situation usually can evoke a "should have" in order to store a "next time I will".

Simulation:

As in computer program, a simulation of an original of something, or a model of an original of something, is a set of concepts, ideas, programs interconnected in such a way as to generate for the thinker — or the reader, the programmer, the programme, a connected whole sufficiently resembling the original something so as to be confused with equal to or identical with the original something. The "connected whole" exists in the program spaces of the reader, the writer, the thinker, the programmer, the programmee. The original something can exist in the external reality, in the internal reality, or both.

We can simulate external systems or internal systems inside our self. Models of thinking-feeling-doing are as valid as models of river drainage systems, of aircraft, of space ships, or of universes.

Supraself:

That aspect of Consciousness-Without-an-Object, of superspace, of essence, which connects with a biocomputer, a bio-self, furnishing information from "networks" and being furnished with information by the biocomputer.

Tape Loop:

A loop of tape in a tape reproducer that repeats a message again and again.

Theoretical Physics:

The experimental science of belief about the universe.

Uncertainty/Indeterminacy:

A belief in our inability to count on, predict, prophesy the future or the future course of a pattern or its changes and the inherently random nature of submicroscopic events as in quantum mechanics are indeterminate. Collapse at a point and re-emergence of a star or a universe are indeterminate.

John C. Lilly, M.D., was a
physician, psychoanalyst and pioneer-
ing scientist in the fields of consciousness,
mind-altering drugs, and animal intelligence. Lilly
conducted studies on solitude, isolation and dolphin-
human relationships. He was associated with the
National Institute of Mental Health (NIMH), and the
Esalen Institute in California. He taught for—or was
affiliated with—CalTech, University of Pennsylvania
School of Medicine, was Associate Professor at the
University of Pennsylvania, and worked in psychoanalysis at the Institute of the Philadelphia Association for Psychoanalysis and Washington-Baltimore
Psychoanalytic Institute and at NIMH. He founded
the Communications Research Institute and in 1954
invented the Isolation Tank Method.

Lilly's work on dolphin intelligence was the subject of a 1973 film, *The Day of the Dolphin*. His work in
developing and experimenting with isolation tanks
was the subject of the 1980 film *Altered States.*

Ronin Books for Independent Minds